REACHING YOUR WORLD

DISCIPLEMAKING FOR WOMEN

BETH MAINHOOD

NAVPRESS ®
A MINISTRY OF THE NAVIGATORS
P.O. Box 6000, Colorado Springs, Colorado 80934

The Navigators is an international Christian organization. Jesus Christ gave His followers the Great Commission to go and make disciples (Matthew 28:19). The aim of The Navigators is to help fulfill that commission by multiplying laborers for Christ in every nation.

NavPress is the publishing ministry of The Navigators. NavPress publications are tools to help Christians grow. Although publications alone cannot make disciples or change lives, they can help believers learn biblical discipleship, and apply what they learn to their lives and ministries.

Unless otherwise identified, all Scripture quotations in this publication are from the *Holy Bible, New International Version* (NIV). Copyright © 1973, 1978, 1984, International Bible Society. Used by permission of Zondervan Bible Publishers. Other versions used: *The New American Standard Bible* (NASB), © 1960, 1973, The Lockman Foundation; the *King James Version* (KJV); and *The New Testament in Modern English, Revised Edition* by J.B. Phillips (PH), © 1958, 1960, 1972 by J.B. Phillips, published by The Macmillan Company, New York.

Printed in the United States of America

Contents

Author

In 1953 Beth Mainhood was doing some counseling for a Billy Graham crusade when she met Dawson Trotman, the founder of The Navigators. Ever since that time in her life, Beth has been dedicated to discipling women in many ways: one-to-one discipling, youth counseling, leading small groups, training women for ministry, and speaking at seminars and conferences.

Beth received a B.S. in Education and an M.A. in Guidance and Counseling from Central Michigan University. She lives in Columbus, Ohio, where she teaches and equips women for ministry.

To Dottie Tupper,
in gratitude for dedicated love
and faithfulness.

CHAPTER ONE

God's Plan for His People

I was desperate. Enough was enough. No one should be expected to go on like this. The bells of my life had tolled. My brain responded to repeated intervals of painful experiences with a clear message: "Without hope, why go on? Why not clear the world of clutter by clearing it of me?"

With those thoughts, I climbed into my car and headed for a nearby highway where the trees stood tall and sturdy. One would do it. "Just hit it hard," I told myself.

But as I was driving my pretty blue car out of the city, several thoughts came to my mind. What would my friends do with all my stuff? And my new car would be such a mess.

And maybe my parents would really miss me. "In fact," I wondered, "how could they explain my actions to the rest of the family?"

I pulled over to the side of the road. My mind was reeling. I put my head on the steering wheel and cried. And cried. "God, where are You?!" I shouted. "Don't You love me? Don't You care?"

Silence. I stopped my crying, and in the calm that followed I took stock of the situation. Something was happening. I realized now that I needed to talk to someone about my despair. Because I could find no reason for why I had been created, I could find no reason for living. But perhaps someone, somewhere, might be able to help me find the reason.

CREATED TO DO GOOD WORKS

With a slight sense of hope, I returned home from my desperate ride. I told no one of my actions, although I did tell a friend that I was greatly discouraged. After a few weeks, I confided in Dottie, a young woman who was to become one of my dearest friends as well as my mentor. During the next few months, she showed me encouraging Scriptures, prayed for me, and communicated in many ways that my life was of substantial value.

One evening we looked at Isaiah 43:7. I was interested to see that God told the people of Israel they were "created for [His] glory." She sent me also to Ephesians 2:10, where I read these words: "We are God's workmanship, created in Christ Jesus to do good works, which God prepared in advance for us to do."

I was startled. Could it be that God wanted *me* to do

good works? Was I really the product of His creation? If so, why was I such a failure? After all, at the age of twenty-four I had already experienced two job failures. That didn't seem to speak too well of the quality of God's craftsmanship. What exactly had He prepared for me to do?

With these questions motivating me, I thoroughly studied those two verses, along with Titus 3:8. Gradually the painful events of the previous year seemed to fade in the face of the brightness of God's words. I had known since childhood that God had created the earth, that it was not just a freak of nature. I knew also that the earth was created as a home for mankind.

But what I had never previously grasped was that the people God chose to be His own had such an important task of *doing His good works*. He calls His people to declare His name, to feed His sheep, to be His witnesses.

This dawning understanding of God's purpose for His people provided the meaning for my own life I had so sorely lacked. During childhood, two great lights came into my life, bringing a measure of meaning and purpose. The first, when I was ten years old, was electricity. It changed our whole family's lifestyle. The kerosene lamp on my bedroom wall was replaced by one light bulb. I immediately noticed the length of the shadows and the intensity of the light. The previously dimly lit room was now brightly lit.

That room symbolizes to me the second great light that came into my life just a year later when I was eleven. The darkness of my spiritual eyes was dispelled by the One who called Himself the Light of the World. As Paul described it in Ephesians 2:3-5, I was dead, in darkness, but because of God's great love I became alive with Christ.

But this new life, good as it was, lacked purpose until my twenty-fourth year. When my friend helped me study in detail those crucial Scripture passages on God's purposes for our lives, my whole outlook on life changed. An eternal reason for living captured my mind and heart: God's people have a significant role in fulfilling His purposes. Personally adopting Ephesians 2:10 enabled me to be His worker.

PROFILES OF WOMEN IN GOD'S BUSINESS

Jesus' parting command to the apostles summarizes the main task of His people. He instructed them to teach others what He had taught them (Matthew 28:18-20). In his fine book *The Master Plan of Evangelism*, Robert Coleman makes the following observation:

> The great commission of Christ given to His Church summed it up in the command to "make disciples of every creature" (Matthew 28:19). The word here indicates that the disciples were to go out into the world and win others who would come to be what they themselves were—disciples of Christ. This mission is emphasized even more when the Greek text of the passage is studied, and it is seen that the words "go," "baptize," and "teach" are all participles which derive their force from the one controlling verb "make disciples."[1]

Because the first disciples of Jesus were actively true to their calling, there are people today who are faithfully helping others come to know God. And as those people know Him in a mature way, they reflect His likeness, obeying "the marching orders that are to be followed until His return."[2]

Women have always taken a significant role in the good works of God's Kingdom business. *All* God's people have a role in His Kingdom work. Unlike a corporation organized to produce tangible gains for the organizers and for some of the privileged participants, God's business is designed to profit all the people who are doing the business (by helping them grow and develop in faith) and also the people who are receiving the benefits of business (by helping them become members of God's family, able to begin reflecting His likeness).

The profile of a woman active in the work of God's Kingdom is recorded in Acts 18. Priscilla was the wife of Aquila, an Italian Jew. They provided a home for Paul in Corinth, where the three of them worked together as tentmakers. Every Sabbath Paul went to the Corinthian synagogue, where he tried to persuade both Jews and Gentiles that Jesus was the Messiah.

Priscilla and Aquila accompanied Paul on his next journey, staying in Ephesus while Paul traveled on to Caesarea. There in Ephesus they had a significant ministry, which included establishing a man named Apollos in his understanding of the gospel and his ability to proclaim it wisely and convincingly. Apollos was "a learned man, with a thorough knowledge of the Scriptures," according to the historian Luke. Although Apollos had already preached boldly and effectively to the Jews, he was still in need of further instruction in the gospel when he arrived in Ephesus. Priscilla and Aquila invited him into their home, where they "explained to him the way of God more adequately."

Luke's account reveals the importance of Priscilla's contribution. She was part of a ministry team with her husband, working alongside and learning from Paul, then putting her experience to work for the believers in Ephesus.

This woman of the early Church was vitally involved in the Great Commission, actively fulfilling God's purposes.

It surprised me that a woman as experienced as Dottie had acquired so many of her skills from the study of Scripture. I had assumed that she was just a natural. But Dottie's story also included a mentor who had opened up the Scriptures for her. After showing me this chapter in Acts, Dottie recounted the spiritual heritage she had received through Joyce and Leila.

As a student nurse, Leila spent many hours explaining to fellow students how they might become members of God's family. She genuinely reflected the image of God in her attitudes and actions. Leila made friends with a young nursing student named Joyce, who had been wanting to know God better ever since her early childhood conversion to Christ. With few exceptions, Leila prayed with Joyce every day for nearly four years; and, as Priscilla and Aquila had done with Apollos, Leila nurtured Joyce in various aspects of her spiritual life.

Following graduation from the university, Leila continued to serve the Kingdom of God with her love, humility, and knowledge of God. She challenged many women to be wholehearted in their relationship with God and to help others do the same. She later married, and with her husband she served the Kingdom of God in several countries until her death in midlife.

After Joyce moved to the city where Dottie was living, she helped women come to know Christ and learn how to reach out to others. She became a loving, faithful mentor to Dottie, who in turn was a loving and faithful mentor to me. Someday heaven's arches will ring with praise to God for what these two women did during their lives on earth. God wants to work *in* women's lives to help them be successful and *through* their lives to help them be purposeful, making an impact on their world. Because of these three women—first Leila, then Joyce, then Dottie—my life was turned around. Their influence continues as I pass on to others what I have experienced, training them to reach out to still more women. The chain goes on and on.

Reading about the life of Gladys Aylward, missionary to China, has challenged me to a greater understanding of the potential for women in God's Kingdom work. Gladys braved a hostile environment in China in order to model God's likeness and give herself to His business. As a young British woman, she faced a tumultuous time in history in order to be available to the Chinese people. Her trip by train across Europe and Asia during the Russian revolution was quite dangerous. Undaunted, Gladys proceeded to a small village where she assisted in reaching China's needy people.

The influence of Gladys was far-reaching. Many children were saved from death by Gladys's ingenious ideas and efforts. A prison riot became a means by which Gladys and her God instituted major changes that subsequently brought help for all of China. People from all walks of life and all ages were welcomed into God's family through her efforts.

Gladys's life has challenged me to persevere, even when all odds seem to be against God and me, until many lost people have an opportunity to come into God's family.

THE OPENING DOORS OF OPPORTUNITY

Can you imagine God creating heaven and earth, and then not wanting people to join Him in His Kingdom? What would the world be like without people? My guess is that the perfect Garden of Eden was a very lonesome place after Adam and Eve left. It had been custom-made for them, but now it was empty, with "a flaming sword flashing back and forth to guard the way to the tree of life" (Genesis 3:24).

God's good earth is filled with people who do their best to prevent God's Kingdom from taking on the semblance of that lonely Eden. In today's world, needs and opportunities for women to do the Kingdom business abound, perhaps in unprecedented fashion. Women are more than ever accessible to the process of being won to the Savior. In America, Europe, and many other regions of the world, women are coming out of their homes into the marketplace. Marvin Harris reports that well over fifty percent of all married American women are working away from their homes on a regular basis.[3] Women are also involved in clubs, associations, and athletic groups. These, plus many other arenas, make excellent "fishing ponds" of evangelism.

The opportunities for taking spiritual advantage of the almost global wind of independence among women appear to be incredible. With this independence may come additional accessibility. This open door complements the long-standing availability of women who spend their days at home. Neighborhood activities to reach this extensive target abound, and have been historically fruitful.

Mobility opens doors. Women are more socially mobile worldwide than in many previous times in history. For example, a village woman from Ghana or Thailand may now achieve a university degree and become a medical doctor or professor. This puts her in places where she may hear of Jesus Christ and become His follower and laborer, thus having the potential to serve Him and the people of His world.

Politically, perhaps never before have the doors been so open to women. In Great Britain, the United States, and other countries, women in political positions are responding positively to caring laborers. One diligent woman laborer in London has in recent years spent countless hours leading Bible studies and discussions with wives of members of Parliament, who in turn greatly influenced others, including their husbands. The women who deal with the pressures and demands of the political arena are a needy group of people. Whether they realize it or not, they are in need of the Savior and all that His loving care can provide.

Notable also is the ability of women to influence men in significant places. My mother used to say, "Man is the head of the family, but woman is the neck that turns the head." That statement may not be totally accurate, but since the days of Eve, we've been generally doing it—sometimes with godly influence, sometimes with ungodly manipulation.

One interesting biblical example of a woman who influenced her husband for good is Samson's mother, who stabilized her fearful husband Manoah with her knowledge of God. Judges 13 records that Manoah and his wife had an encouraging piece of news from an angel of the Lord. Manoah's wife had been barren, a cultural shame in those days. But the news from the angel was that she would "conceive and give birth to a son." After some discussion, the angel departed in a miraculous flourish. This encounter frightened Manoah, who rightly concluded that the angel was from the Lord. "We're as good as dead," he said to his wife, "because we have seen God." But his wife carefully responded, "If God had targeted us for death, He would never have accepted our offerings. And He wouldn't have let us know all these things, especially now" (my paraphrase).

After these reassuring words from his wife, Manoah apparently had no more fearful questions. Prepared as she was through her knowledge of God, Manoah's wife was a healthy source of encouragement to him. He realized that he *needed* her.

A recent publication by Overseas Missionary Fellowship recounts brief biographies of several women who have significantly influenced people, many of them men, as we saw in the case of Priscilla. These men's lives were perceptibly affected by the bold witness of these women. As I read *Each to Her Post* by Phyllis Thompson, I prayed that all of today's women and those of tomorrow would take seriously their task of positively building up the men in their lives. God calls women to this labor of love, and men truly need that female support in their lives.

The purpose of this book is to help women become functioning laborers—women who will pray for our land, modeling and sharing their faith by opening their hearts and homes to responsive people. There are so few men and women in the world who know how to combine living and laboring. Most people give their time and energy strictly to the tangible things in life. Their jobs, the house and the lawn, cooking and cars, take priority over sharing their faith, leading a Bible study, or some other aspect of spiritual laboring. Somewhere the idea was invented that only fulltime, professional church employees are to do those tasks. But it has always been God's intention that all believers labor in the context of their daily lives. There is a far greater need worldwide for lay laborers than for professional leaders. God brings people into His family through *all* His dedicated laboring people.

NOTES
1. Robert E. Coleman, *The Master Plan of Evangelism* (Westwood, N.J.: Fleming H. Revell, 1963), page 108.
2. James F. Engel and H. Wilbert Norton, *What's Gone Wrong with the Harvest?* (Grand Rapids: Zondervan, 1975), page 43.
3. Chapter 5 of Marvin Harris's book *America Now: The Anthropology of a Changing Culture* (New York: Simon & Schuster, 1981) gives an interesting sociological account of several aspects of American women in the twentieth century.

FOR PERSONAL DEVELOPMENT

Use Isaiah 43:4-7, 58:10-12, and Ephesians 2:10 in order to work through the following exercises:

1. Rewrite these verses in your own words.
2. Ask questions about these passages using the words *what, when, where, why,* and *how.*
   Example: What is the meaning of "precious"?
3. Answer the most important of the questions you wrote.
4. Memorize one of the above Scripture passages that best states your purpose in life.
5. Write a prayer to God about your findings.

Optional: Read Ruth, looking for ways Naomi helped Ruth become a woman of God.

CHAPTER TWO

A Philosophy of Ministry

God is constantly calling people to come into His family to be His laborers. Dedicated women laborers will never want for a task, for someone to need them, for personal significance. But what basic philosophy of ministry should women pursue? Where do we find a solid foundation and guideline for laboring? Certainly a lifelong involvement in the Kingdom ministry will be truly effective only when it is soundly based on Scripture.

Philosophy is the search for principles of reality. A ministry is godly and effective only when based on the realities of God. Laborers need to inquire into the most comprehensive principles of these realities. We need to know as much as God wants to tell us.

The word *philosophy* is the combination of two Greek words meaning "love of wisdom." The best way to gain wisdom is to search for it. Scripture *is* wisdom. No godly ministry would be complete without a foundation in the truth of God's Word. During my years as a laborer, I have learned so much from searching the Scriptures. I have received messages from God with great eagerness, examining the Scriptures every day, as the Bereans did, to see what is true (Acts 17:11).

The first chapter of 2 Corinthians contains several notes of great significance to a philosophy of ministry. From this chapter we can draw several essential principles on which we can base our ministry.

Principle one: Our message of caring must be given to others consistently (2 Corinthians 1:15-18).

In his second epistle to the Corinthians, Paul emphasized the importance of consistency in his communication to them. "I planned to visit you first so that you might benefit twice. . . . When I planned this, did I do it lightly? Or do I make my plans in a worldly manner so that in the same breath I say, 'Yes, yes' and 'No, no'?" (2 Corinthians 1:15-18).

When we flip-flop our love signals, we violate the dignity of Christ's love. Jesus was consistent in His love for people. He cared equally for the rich young ruler (Matthew 19), the Samaritan woman (John 4), and His betrayer, Judas. To illustrate the importance of consistency, a funny story from my often not-so-funny experiences comes to my mind.

In a neighborhood where I once lived, there were two small children, one on either side of my house. From my very first day in the house, I looked for ways to share love and the truth of the gospel with the children's mothers. I prayed for them, expressed verbally that I cared about them, and did many little acts of friendship for them.

On a day in the last week of July one year, I noticed that about twenty small green peppers had ripened on three plants in my back yard—in the morning that I looked, that is. In the evening, there were sixteen dying green peppers lying on the ground, each the victim of one bite from some curious passersby.

Almost by instinct I knew who the curious tasters were. But that posed a dilemma for me. Could I prove my hunch? Would the mothers think I cared more about green peppers than about them and their children? As I viewed the situation, my prayer was, "Father, thank You for all the ways You have let me show and speak of Your love to these families. Please guard that love, and help me know what to do. And thank You that people are more important than green peppers."

About an hour later I heard voices outside the dining room window. There stood the two neighbor children, each with a pepper missing a bite-size quantity. Now I had to face the question because the guilty parties were caught green-handed. After a silent "Lord, thanks and help!" I went outside to confront my two little friends.

Following a brief discussion, I took each by the empty hand, and walked them to their mothers. Not only was my heart pounding, but I could almost hear theirs, too. As I knocked at the first door, I felt a sense of quietness come over me, knowing God was going to use this humorous episode for good. And He did, much to my immense joy.

Both mothers were glad that I came to them, and thanked me for being a faithful friend. One even sent her son back the next day to apologize. He gave me three large peppers, paid for from his allowance. The mother had interpreted my caring as consistent, for which I thanked God. We need to make our message a Christlike yes, not a confusing yes and no (2 Corinthians 1:17-20).

> *Principle two: The major source of our ministry is Jesus Christ (2 Corinthians 1:18-20).*

Paul's major theme was Jesus because He was the primary affirmative, guiding force in the apostle's life. Paul said, "The Son of God, Jesus Christ, who was preached among you by me and Silas and Timothy, was not 'Yes' and 'No,' but in him it has always been 'Yes'" (2 Corinthians 1:19).

Only one person can be the originator of a ministry that pleases God: Jesus Christ. This Jesus exhibited love in all its supremacy, forgiveness in all its power, and humility in all its radiance. With the coming of Jesus, the world received grace and truth, new concepts for a law-oriented society.

We care because Christ cared. We can proclaim to the world that the caring Redeemer has come, that God's promises have been fulfilled. He is the One who gives people a sharing relationship. Only Christ can use our adherence to the Bible to bring God glory.

I like the verses in 2 Corinthians 4:5-6 that drive home the concept that Jesus is our source of ministry:

> We do not preach ourselves, but Jesus Christ as Lord, and ourselves as your servants for Jesus' sake. For God, who

said, "Let light shine out of darkness," made his light
shine in our hearts to give us the light of the knowledge of
the glory of God in the face of Christ.

I never proclaim myself to anyone, but I do proclaim Christ
Jesus as Lord. We see the glory of God in the face of Christ.
Our strength and vision come from His life. Our persist-
ence originates in His grace.

*Principle three: The major content of our ministry is
the Word of God (2 Corinthians 1:20).*

Paul reminded the Corinthians that God's promises
recorded in Scripture were affirmed in Christ. "For no
matter how many promises God has made, they are 'Yes' in
Christ. And so through him the 'Amen' is spoken by us to
the glory of God" (2 Corinthians 1:20).

In Scripture we have the resources needed both to
learn for ourselves and to give to others. Timothy was
charged by his faithful mentor Paul to persist in the Scriptures, because "all Scripture is God-breathed and is useful
for teaching, rebuking, correcting and training in righteousness, so that the man of God may be thoroughly
equipped for every good work" (2 Timothy 3:14-17).

In Matthew 19:16-22 there is an excellent example of
how Jesus used Scripture as the content and guideline of
His ministry. The heart of His reply to the rich young ruler
was Deuteronomy 5:16-20 and Leviticus 19:18, scriptural
quotations strategically chosen in order to confront the
man's self-righteousness.

*Principle four: God establishes the relationships through
which good works are ministered (2 Corinthians 1:21).*

Paul stated, "It is God who makes both us and you stand firm in Christ" (2 Corinthians 1:21). Both the laborer and the recipient of the labor are established by God. *The New American Standard Bible* renders this verse, "Now He who establishes us with you in Christ and anointed us is God." We can and should do all the right things to relate to people, but it is by the grace and power of God alone that these efforts are brought to fruition.

> *Principle five: The laborer may need to change plans for the sake of the person she is ministering to (2 Corinthians 1:23).*

Sensitivity to people and circumstances is essential in ministry. Paul was willing to change his plans when he realized that his visit would be quite difficult on the Corinthians. In his letter to them Paul stated, "It was in order to spare you that I did not return to Corinth" (2 Corinthians 1:23).

A lifestyle that is flexible illustrates love to those we want to serve. A person who labors for God is always on call. Because our top priority is God's Kingdom, we need to be sensitive to the changing needs within that Kingdom (Matthew 6:33). Putting God's concerns first in our life ensures that we will receive all we need. We need to be flexible enough to do *God's* will. Such a flexible lifestyle is costly, but the end result is a great eternal reward.

> *Principle six: The laborer is not a master, but a helper (2 Corinthians 1:24).*

Paul had no desire to push people around. He expressed to the Corinthians, "Not that we lord it over your faith, but we work with you for your joy, because it is by faith you stand firm" (2 Corinthians 1:24).

A person doesn't need to take control of someone else to be a laborer. We are called to co-labor with other people and with the Holy Spirit of God. If we had to be overlords or total rulers, we would have to assume the intolerable burden of complete responsibility for all actions and attributes. As helpers we can assist. As masters we would control. The laborer should not be what is both useless and detrimental.

> *Principle seven: The people we minister to stand by faith (2 Corinthians 1:24).*

"It is by faith you stand firm." When people come to Christ, they come with faith that He will forgive them, love them, and give them eternal life. Then as Christ's disciples, they follow Him also by faith. The laborer will be success-ful *only* when faith is a significant part of the disciple's growth process.

If the laborer exerts more effort than faith, then nega-tive results may follow. Even though we may intend to help, we often end up hindering.

WHAT NOT TO DO

How should a laborer for Christ help a new believer? Well, I learned the hard way how *not* to help. I remember a particular time when I was trying to help a young believer in the early stages of her relationship with God. I discov-ered that she was dating a nonChristian and that they had serious thoughts of marriage. I confronted her very directly one day: "Don't you know God doesn't want you to date an unbeliever?"

My friend was offended by my words and became defensive. Her response—that she *liked* him—carried by strong inference the message that I was to mind my own affairs. I resisted her message, mentioning instead the name of a young Christian man who would be more right for her, according to my thinking. I was aware that this other young man really liked her.

The conversation came to an immediate halt when she walked out of the room in anger after I had made the suggestion that she give him a chance. Her parting words— "I won't!"—ring in my ears to this day. She apparently decided then and there to make sure I minded my own business. She was no longer open to my help.

As a laborer, I cared; I had a mother's concern. *But* I did not demonstrate my concern out of a belief that she walked by faith. My belief was that *I* needed to straighten out her thinking and actions. I ended up smothering her and eventually lost any opportunities to be her friend and mentor. How much better it is to grasp the reality of Scripture: "Neither he who plants nor he who waters is anything, but only God, who makes things grow" (1 Corinthians 3:7).

The seemingly endless truth is that there is plenty of spiritual work to be done—"but the workers are few" (Matthew 9:37). This fact first became evident in Noah's day, when his was the only God-fearing family on earth. And Abraham couldn't find enough righteous people in Sodom and Gomorrah to prevent the destruction of the cities by a torrent of fire and brimstone. Ezekiel reported that not one person could be found to pray for the land (Ezekiel 22:30).

Jesus said to His disciples, "The harvest is plentiful but the workers are few. Ask the Lord of the harvest, therefore, to send out workers into his harvest field" (Matthew 9:37-38). After nearly two thousand years this is still the case: There are very few laborers who are willing to work in the business of God's Kingdom. But that's no excuse for us. It is our challenge to motivate and equip people for God's work in the harvest field. With a solid philosophy of ministry and the willingness to serve our Lord, we are well on our way as women of the Kingdom toward reaching the world for the King.

FOR PERSONAL DEVELOPMENT

1. Principles are comprehensive and fundamental assumptions. Can you find any other Scriptures that support or confirm the ministry principles drawn out of 2 Corinthians?
2. Look back at the seven principles listed in this chapter, and then read through the first chapter of 2 Corinthians. Are there any other ministry principles that you think should be included in the list?
3. What obstacles may keep you from becoming a functioning laborer? After listing them, ask someone you trust to pray against these obstacles.

CHAPTER THREE

Stages of Growth

The physical world has much to offer the careful observer. A sunset mirrored by a lake, twilight overtaking a grain field—feasts for the eyes! The mating call of the cardinal and water spilling over rocks are forms of music to the ear. For those who want to learn, the changing seasons remind us of how temporary life on this earth is, and the rolling oceans pound out the power of God, Master of this physical world and all it contains.

When spring flowers begin to brighten our yards, we are again reminded that growing is a privilege—sometimes painful, but always productive. My tulips rarely escape a spring snow bath. Surely those lovely white snowflakes must cause pain to the fine tissue of the tulips, but the flowers never seem to complain. They just sit there bravely, growing in the midst of hardship. Sometimes I'm tempted to ask God if He is perhaps forgetting about the tulips when He scatters the snowflakes. But these flowers, privileged once more to see the light of day after months in an underground dwelling, endure pain in order to produce their colorful blossoms—and perhaps to attract the attention of a pensive observer.

These lessons on growth from the earth can help challenge the woman laborer to take personal responsibility for her own growth. The growing person will be the giving person; the stagnant person will have nothing to share with the one she could otherwise help. Isaiah wrote about this issue in a recorded conversation with Hezekiah. He said, "Once more a remnant of the house of Judah will take root below and bear fruit above" (Isaiah 37:31). As Judah established herself as a nation of God, she revealed her God-centeredness to others. This illustration goes along with Jesus' statement to His disciples in John 15:4: "Remain in me, and I will remain in you. No branch can bear fruit by itself; it must remain in the vine. Neither can you bear fruit unless you remain in me."

Our relationship to God is like the branches on the vine. Sometimes the branches are tested by the elements. But as we mature in our grasp and application of God's heart-borne truths, we reveal our organic relationship with Him to our world. The privilege of growth in Godlikeness is painful at times, but always productive.

There are at least three basic responsibilities—like those of the tulip bulbs, from which beautiful petals eventually grow. These responsibilities position us for growth.

First, *we should develop and maintain an intimate rela-tionship with God.* Second, *we should try to live a bal-anced, available life.* Third, *we need to be sure to get under the spiritual umbrella of someone else's guidance.* Let's take a look at these three responsibilities in some detail.

Most believers desire a deep personal relationship with God, including the sense of intimacy often associated with an ultimate achievement in relating. But sometimes we fail to grasp our part in becoming familiar with His nature and actions. Other times we don't comprehend how significant it is to Him and us when there is a failure in communication or some other rift in the relationship. This meaningful, love-centered relationship with God can grow as we spend time with Him, developing trust in Him and learning how to both understand and grasp His direction for us.

It might be helpful for you to make a good evaluation of the devotional life you have already established. See what steps you can take to improve this key relationship. From this relationship with God will come insights, ideas, heart, and vision to help others.

One evening I was scheduled to lead a small Bible study group. That day I had been out of sorts with God, with myself, and—obvious to others—with most people. My "logical" solution to the problem was to skip Bible study . . . "because I'm not fit to lead it."

When I voiced my intent and rationale to my mentor, she challenged me with a few concise words, carefully chosen: "Why can't you make things right with God, and then go? Do you think He can help you?"

My logic couldn't refute her challenge. I took her words and my attitude up to my room, where God and I had a little talk about matters. When the time came for me to leave for the Bible study, I was ready.

How can we help others grow if we don't grow our-selves? It takes maturity to function from a good con-science, from the teachings of God's Word, from faith, from love. And only by keeping our walk, our way, our life with God current and open can any growth take place.

If we want to help people, we need to be available—to whatever degree God leads. This is equally true for the single person as for the married person, although the nature of that availability may differ.

The single woman may need reminders that to be available doesn't mean becoming a superwoman. She needs to use wise judgment about how many people she can help, how many hours her job can take, how much time it takes just to live.

On the flip side, however, her singleness doesn't mean that she owns her life. When Paul discussed the rights of an apostle in 1 Corinthians 9, he qualified those rights by saying, "Though I am free and belong to no man, I make myself a slave to everyone, to win as many as possible" (9:19). In another letter, he spelled it out this way: "For none of us lives to himself alone and none of us dies to himself alone. If we live, we live to the Lord; and if we die, we die to the Lord. So, whether we live or die, we belong to the Lord" (Romans 14:7-8).

Paul continued his discussion of an apostle's rights with a very helpful explanation. "For this very reason," he pointed out, "Christ died and returned to life so that he might be the Lord of both the dead and the living" (Romans 14:9). If we choose to live only for ourselves, we are in direct opposition to the very reason for which Christ came, and eventually died.

The married woman may have different time considerations for helping others than the single woman. She will want to set proper priorities in agreement with her husband for scheduling her time. This will prevent conflicts of interest that come because priorities have not been defined and agreed on.

Vitally important for both married and single women is thoughtful but not fanatical health care. Our bodies belong to God (1 Corinthians 6:19-20). Some things are investments, not expenses. Those habits that keep our health as stable as possible are an investment in availability. Good diet, sleep patterns, exercise, and attitude toward the need for these disciplines will benefit not only ourselves but also the ministries of the Kingdom.

One lesson I learned fairly early in my life speaks to the other side of this issue: God also uses the person who is physically limited. My grandmother spent her last three years in a hospital. During much of that time she shared a room with a woman who, because of a stroke, was totally paralyzed. All she could move was her head and, because of God's grace, her spiritual heart. She prayed, she shared, and she served. In one situation, she prayed for a nurse to come help my grandmother, and one came hurrying in, although neither of the two women had pushed the call button. Her physical disability did not limit her spiritual capability.

It is not necessary to be a superwoman to help people grow in Christ. What it takes is a person who will pray, "Here I am, God. Because of Your grace in my life I want to serve You. Where do I begin?"

A careful study of Scripture reveals that people who help others spiritually are accountable not only to a leader but also to each other. A protective spiritual umbrella—a person or a group who holds us accountable, encourages us, and challenges us—is spiritually vital. When we help others, we become a part of the protection they need. We, too, need that kind of interpersonal protection.

METHODS

The process of establishing potential laborers calls for several methods. These various methods can be used in many ways, depending on the person's stage of growth.

We could easily compare the spiritual growth process, which I am referring to as *establishing*, to that of the physical child's maturation. Just as a mother uses one method of communicating with her son when he is six months old and another method when he is six years old, so the spiritually young believer requires different methods of communication at different time periods.

In the physical realm of life, growth begins with birth and moves sequentially through infancy, childhood, adolescence, and adulthood. Each of these stages is marked by certain characteristics and needs. Some are visible, others invisible. The stages also overlap. The spiritual growth process can be compared to these stages of physical maturation. The woman who first puts her life in God's hands, having experienced a new birth, is called a convert. The stages of growth then move successively, resulting eventually in the maturity needed to reproduce spiritual children.

The writer of Hebrews had this progressive maturity in mind. He was very concerned about his readers not turning their backs on the teachings about Jesus. He chided them for not being able to take all he had to say. Instead of being responsible and mature in their faith, they still needed milk. He concluded with this analysis: "Anyone who lives on milk, being still an infant, is not acquainted with the teaching about righteousness. But solid food is for the mature, who by constant use have trained themselves to distinguish good from evil" (Hebrews 5:13-14).

He continued in 6:1, "Therefore let us leave the elementary teachings about Christ and go on to maturity," encouraging them to stop returning to the rudiments of the faith and to begin ingesting solid food. He optimistically concluded, "And God permitting, we will do so" (6:3). The writer of Hebrews saw that there were stages in the process of growth, and he longed for his audience to keep moving through those stages to maturity. We, too, should long for our people to grow to fruitful spiritual adulthood—not to remain in infancy or childhood.

Each step or time frame of growth requires particular methods in order for learning to take place. For example, while the mother of a six-month-old infant transmits love not through class sessions but through physical and emotional nurture, the mother of an adolescent may express love through consistent discipline.

These principles apply to the establishing process. Here are three types of methods that I have found effective for establishing young believers:

1. Structured or Planned

Purpose: To teach and transmit systematically to the new believer the biblical truths necessary for his growth into the next stage.[1]

Setting: A place where prayer and God's Word can be shared with openness and confidence on a regular basis.

Methods: One-to-one and small group discussions.

Content: Centered around long-range objectives; designed to meet immediate goals; planned to develop skills and attitudes; Bible-centered and relevant to the believer's stage of growth.

2. Unstructured or Freestyle

Purpose: To develop the establishing relationship in a freestyle way that results in mutual learning and growth for both the laborer and the young disciple; to contribute to the best overall development objectives for the disciple.

Setting: Any place where an informal conversation can be carried on, such as over a cup of coffee.

Methods: One-to-one; impromptu dinner conversations; planned time to discuss an unplanned topic or outline.

Content: Feedback from structured times; responses to life's experiences; questions discussed on various issues; spontaneous reading of the Scriptures and prayer.

3. Recreational or Relaxational

Purpose: To win the heart, making friendship an integral part of the establishing relationship; to demonstrate a Christlike, balanced life; to make observations that will help in planning for the disciple's growth.

Setting: A golf course, decoupage room, athletic area, or any place where a casual atmosphere exists.

Methods: One-on-one or group observations; conversations; questions and answers; sharing life stories; listening.

Content: Primarily the work of God's Spirit using the activities in both persons' lives.

The establishing examples from Jesus recorded in the Gospels have many variations. Jesus taught people in creative ways, both individually and in groups. He knew better than to bore His followers with dry lectures.

The three principles of establishing—maintaining an intimate relationship with God, living a balanced, available life, and receiving guidance from a spiritual mentor—may be applied creatively during the following stages of spiritual growth:

Stage 1: Infancy—Use a loose application of the structured method along with the freestyle and recreational methods.

Just as newborn babies need a planned diet of food, physical care, love, and nurture, so newborn baby Christians need spiritual food that is planned and prepared for their individual needs.

Stage 2: Childhood—Use a somewhat strict application of the structured method along with the freestyle and recreational methods.

Growing children need regular, systematic teaching. They also need time to talk with their parents and time to play together. Paul used the parent-child relationship as a model for spiritual growth (1 Thessalonians 2:9-13).

Stage 3: Adolescence—Use less of the structured method and more of the freestyle and the recreational methods.

Adolescents need their parents to continue teaching them, but at the same time they need the freedom to learn in more indirect ways. This same principle also applies to spiritual adolescents.

Stage 4: Adulthood—Use a lot of the freestyle and recreational methods with a little of the structured method.

With a combination of these three methods, co-laborship can blossom as the disciple moves into her own ministry of helping others become spiritual adults.

In John 21, an interesting dialogue takes place. Note that Jesus tells Peter at first to feed the lambs and later He calls for the sheep to be fed. This illustrates a vital point about the growth process: Lambs do become sheep. The following chart summarizes how this maturation concept is applied to the establishing process.

THE ESTABLISHING PROCESS

Physical growth stage	Infancy	Childhood	Adolescence	Adulthood
Growth status	Convert	Christian Child	Christian Adolescent	Christian Adult
Level of learning	Stage 1	Stage 2	Stage 3	Stage 4
Establishing method	Loosely structured, freestyle, recreation	Structured, freestyle, recreation	Lessening structure, freestyle, recreation	Diminished structure, freestyle, recreation

As this chart points out, all four stages of growth use the same three kinds of methods. The starting point for the Christian who wants to grow may help to determine which kind will best serve a need. For example, a person who believed in Christ five years earlier but had never grown at all may desire to make up for lost time with a rapid pace. On the other hand, a brand new believer who has never had much Bible orientation and is unaccustomed to learning directly from other people may need to be helped through more recreational, freestyle means. Short discussions after a racquetball game for a few weeks may be the best technique for helping to overcome the barrier of her reserve.

People respond to the establishing principles in very unexpected ways. I've known some new believers to actively and fervently pursue their shepherds for help. After Jesus removed their sin and the ensuing guilt, they hungered and longed for the Scriptures, for time to talk and pray. The starting point included not only their history, but also the degree of their need. People who sense their need for God and His Word usually put forth the most effort to grow.

Because all people are different, they need to be accepted for who they are, not rejected because they aren't like someone else. If all children skipped their teen years, life might be more peaceful—but it certainly would be incomplete. The same is true with spiritual growth. As we visualize others' potential for growth and commit ourselves to making it possible for them, we become enablers of this growth.

When I first began to help Mickie grow, she was seventeen and a fairly new believer. One of her high school teachers had helped her on her path to becoming a Christian. This same teacher was also my mentor prior to the beginning of my shepherding relationship with Mickie. After our first conversation, I knew that Mickie was hungry for God and that I'd have to learn a lot in order to help her grow. This insight motivated me to trust God for a deeper relationship with Him, knowing that Mickie would be observing my life.

It was also a challenge to me to be available to her on a regular basis. We met almost every week for talks about God, the Bible, and her life. We would go swimming, then talk. She was in a Bible study that I led, where we had meaningful group discussions. We both grew as God used His Word along with our efforts. I called my pastor, requesting prayer for my ability to be a godly shepherd and mentor. This spiritual umbrella protected me, and the prayers were answered.

Thus I was able to use various means to help Mickie grow. I joyfully watched as she made steady progress through the various stages of spiritual maturity. Just two years had passed since my disillusionments and fears had driven me to a near disaster. Now the purposes of God were being fulfilled in my life, and the reality of His promises were evident. I had *hope* at last! Life lived for others was well worth living.

NOTES
1. Some good NavPress materials on Bible study and Scripture memorization:

> *Design for Discipleship* (7-book Bible study series with leader's guide)
> *Studies in Christian Living* (9-book Bible study series with leader's guide)
> *Think It Through* by George Howard (follow-up Bible study)
> *Topical Memory System* (complete Scripture memory system)
> *Scripture Memory Packs* (each of these eight topical packs contains 36 key passages).

These NavPress materials are available through NavPress, P.O. Box 6000, Colorado Springs, Colorado 80934, or your local Christian bookstore.

For Personal Development

1. Think through the various aspects of your relationship toward God, such as your love and respect for Him, and your disciplines of daily devotions, Scripture memory, and prayer. What do you desire in your relationship? What are God's responsibilities and what are yours?
2. Do you need to do anything to become more available to God?
3. What characteristics do you see in each Physical Growth and Spiritual Growth stage? (See chart on page 40.) What are some methods you would use to help someone move from childhood into adolescence? From adolescence into adulthood?
4. Read Hebrews 5:11-6:3. What do you observe in this passage about growth in general?
5. Write a short prayer thanking God for all the people in your life who have helped you grow in Christlikeness.

CHAPTER FOUR

Reaching Out to Others

Phyllis McGinley, a gifted writer from New England, once said, "A woman is never happier than when she's giving herself away." This statement could just as easily have been mine because I, like many people, thrive on being needed. It is a great privilege to know for certain that I am significant to someone.

The safest way to fulfill this desire to be needed is to become an instrument in the hand of God. There are many precious women in the world who could become laborers if someone would win them to Christ, establish them in their faith, and help them become instruments of God. Women are needed to give themselves away—to the work of God's Kingdom.

The neediest women in the world are those without Jesus in their lives. Their need is so great because their position is so precarious. They are only a breath away from a Christless eternity, and one breath is such a short span of time. All of today's laborers were once in this same precarious state before they were brought into the family of God. People were the primary instruments through which His Spirit led them.

Millions of potential laborers can be found among either nonbelievers or believers. When we find people who are without Jesus, we can be instrumental in leading them to Him as their Savior, and then taking them further down the pathway of service. When we find people who are already believers, we can help them see their potential for service as laborers.

UNBELIEVERS

Unbelievers are brought into the family of God as He draws them and as they respond to the Holy Spirit who is convicting them of sin. Usually, but not always, unbelievers are attracted to God through the life messages of Christians. These messages are conveyed both verbally and nonverbally.[1]

As an instrument of God, a Christian can attract people to God by demonstrating love, mercy, righteousness, and integrity. Ordinary people who are Christlike become extraordinary as they have to serve within the cauldron of the world. The true story of a woman named Thelma illustrates this powerful truth. Thelma was an unbeliever who happened to notice a profound difference in a friend. Thelma saw her friend's forgiving spirit, her willingness to be corrected when wrong, and her prompt return from lunch breaks.

This kind of behavior intrigued her. "Why don't you lose your temper when things go wrong?" Thelma asked her friend one day.

"Well, usually I ask God to help me, Thelma," her friend responded, "and He does. Sometimes, however, I do become angry, and then I ask God to help me control it."

Thelma looked at her a minute, then walked away, shaking her head and muttering, "I don't understand."

A few days later, after her friend had spent some time praying for Thelma, there was another exchange. The friend was anxious to help Thelma become a believer, but she didn't want to offend her in the process by being too forceful. "What should I do?" she wondered.

"Thelma," she said one morning, "would you be interested in joining a Bible study discussion group? You could learn more about how to develop the life qualities we were talking about the other day."

Thelma's response was positive. "How'd you get interested in all these things about God anyway?" she queried.

That question gave her friend an opening to share both her own brief testimony and a visual illustration of how to become a Christian. Thelma took the illustration home with her, much to her friend's delight. More prayer, more demonstrations of Christlikeness, and one day, several weeks later after a Bible study discussion, Thelma put her life into the hands of God.

This new Christian represented another potential laborer. Her neediness helped break down the barrier of pride, and her friend was able to cooperate with God, the

Bible study leader, and Thelma herself to assist in her new birth.

A story like this one can be multiplied many times over. Neighbors, relatives, associates on the job—there are people everywhere who do not know the Lord. God reaches out to others through us, His followers. As you reach out to develop a meaningful relationship with unbelievers, think of them as potential instruments of God.

BELIEVERS

One approach that is often very helpful is to take a good, hard look at all your acquaintances before you determine where to begin. Ask yourself, Which young or new believers might want to grow in Christ, if given the opportunity? Are any of these women close enough in proximity, interests, and spiritual age to join together for a Bible study discussion? Is there just one who might respond if I took the initiative to try to help her on a personal basis?

When I first began to think about this idea of helping others grow, I hardly knew what to do. So I prayed. And I prayed. And I prayed!

Prayer number one: "God, how can I help women? Almost everyone I know is smarter than I am. They're better educated. They probably won't like me, let alone allow me to help them. Maybe this just isn't my thing."

"So much for that idea," I told myself, "I'm not going to try something that is so uncertain, so risky. I'll give my time to my job, and forget it all."

But the next day, I was drawn by the power of love to pray again. Prayer number two: "God," I started, "forget what I told You yesterday. I *do* want to try to help women grow in Christ, but I don't know how. I don't even know where to start. Would You help me?"

At that moment I had a better sense of peace that somewhere, someday, someone would want me to be her shepherd.

By faith, I prayed prayer number three: "God, thank You for faithfully holding my hand, and for not letting me run away from Your assignment. Would You please help Ann and Janet want me to help them? Would You please give me wisdom and courage to approach them about being in a Bible study discussion? Thanks! I need all the help I can get."

Because I already had a friendship with Ann and Janet, I could let God enable me to use our friendship as a beginning of a helping relationship. I had asked the question, Who wants to grow? and found the answer in an existing friendship.

Along with the search among acquaintances and friends, some people have found it helpful to use an informative prayer chart. We may not know for sure where people are in their growth process. But presenting ideas to God and asking for His prospering touch will be a safe venture. The prayer chart might look like this:

Potential Laborers

Nonbelievers	Young Christians
Jane	Laura
Susy	Denise
Tanya	Kathy
Lisa	Betty
	Diane
	Sherrie

For evangelistic efforts, start with the unbelievers who seem to be closest to believing. If you're not sure about their attitude toward God, assume that they are interested but uninformed and then make every effort to bring them into God's family.

If the young believers are all from one church or have a common meeting ground such as place of employment, professional association, or neighbors in one given area, you can gather them together for group establishing. Decide on an evening for a meeting, and then consider extending the invitation either by telephone or by letter. When you make the invitation, explain the purpose, the initial duration of the group, and the requirements. Remember that some people are more attracted to a leader who presents herself as someone who is learning along with the participants.

RECRUITING

To start recruiting the available, the hungry, and the needy, I suggest building a relationship that is comprised of love, honesty, and a willingness to try to help. This relationship can serve the shepherding process in the same way that a platform provides a concert performer with a means of communication. You can make suggestions, offer to pray, ask questions, and give feedback.

Many people are reticent about taking the initiative in building relationships, but when others come to them, they respond. As instruments of God, we must be willing to give without waiting for others to give back. Paul told the Corinthians, "I will very gladly spend for you everything I have and expend myself as well. If I love you more, will you love me less?" (2 Corinthians 12:15). He was willing to give the Corinthians all he had of himself even though, as the *King James Version* puts it, "The more abundantly I love you, the less I be loved."

This essential willingness to be spent for others draws attention to our need to keep our relationship with God very personal and current. Without a steady supply of God's grace and love flowing into a life that is being constantly emptied through giving to others, a laborer could easily become dry, perhaps hardened, and possibly useless. Without God's enabling we become impatient, giving up because change takes so long.

This lesson became clear to me during a period of time when I tried to help a person who rejected much of what I offered her. Since the struggle was so great, my inclination was to stop trying to help that woman grow. But I couldn't ignore that verse—2 Corinthians 12:15. Was I willing to spend and be spent? Was I more concerned about her or me?

One night I walked the floor of my room discussing the whole issue with God. Several things became clear after those moments in prayer:

1. God was truly concerned about her growth.
2. Only He could use me as an instrument.
3. An instrument needs to be available to be of value.
4. I couldn't force my ideas on her, but I could faithfully offer my help, stopping only when she refused it.
5. The grace of God would help me help her.

My contribution to her was of limited duration and content, but later, as I pondered the whole situation, I knew I'd done what pleased God. Not all experiences will be precisely like that one, but some might be. The best way to prepare for possible refusal is to commit the process to God and take only as much responsibility as He gives.

Prayer is a significant part of our ministry to others. It could be identified as the frame for the platform, the beginning structure on which the boards are laid. We might refer to the boards as verbal interaction. As a recruiting relationship is being developed, you can share personal needs or lessons you have learned or are now learning. You can also ask for prayer for daily concerns.

The objective of the recruiting process is for the person who is being recruited to allow herself to be helped to some degree. To allow this help, she needs to know that she is cared for. She must be able to share confidences, knowing that they will be honored. She needs to view her shepherd not as a domineering person but as a friend who is being used by God to enhance her life.

With this objective in mind, the nails used to keep the boards on the frame could be deeds of kindness. It is an act of kindness, for example, to become interested in things that are important to others. One lady I helped for a while was interested in ceramics. This was not my idea of a fun craft, but for her sake and Jesus' sake, I spent time learning about it. Then, from this common interest, our relationship was improved and she allowed me to help her.

Other examples of kind deeds? How about planning a simple picnic together, writing a short note, or making a little gift? Even a casual phone call can be an expression of caring. Whatever expresses the idea of gentle consideration, goodwill, or a favorable spirit will help prayer and verbal interaction serve as a platform, a relationship from which we can minister.

We do not need to wait for perfection in our lives and skills before starting to help. Through prayer, verbal interaction, and deeds of kindness, a potential laborer can construct a ministry, serving others as a kindhearted shepherd.

AN EXAMPLE

When Dorothy first started to help Barb, she offered to pray with her about a small issue or concern. That was on Sunday.

Then came Wednesday evening. The phone rang in Barb's home.

"Hello, Barb? This is Dorothy. Do you have a minute?"

"Yes, I have two in fact!"

"Well," Dorothy swallowed hard and continued, "I was wondering how things went with you today regarding your decision."

Barb was somewhat taken aback. She was not accustomed to anyone asking her about her personal concerns. But she responded with a short answer.

"I just wanted you to know, Barb, that I'll keep praying," Dorothy answered her. "Is there any other aspect of this situation that I can pray with you about?"

"Yes," Barb answered. "I'm not sure who I should try to please in the matter. And I haven't any way of knowing."

At this point Dorothy could easily have given her a short lesson on pleasing God, but instead she opted to remember her question, "What can I pray for?" not, "What can I teach you?"

"Oh, Barb, I'll be glad to pray with you about that," was her eager reply. "You can count on it."

"Thanks, Dorothy."

"Sure, Barb. We'll talk later. Take care. 'Bye."

Following this brief conversation, Dorothy prayed, as she had promised. In a few days she called Barb again. After a brief exchange, during which she learned that Barb was still in a quandary about whom to please, Dorothy took the next step in helping Barb: offering to meet with her to look at Scripture for direction about whom she should please. Barb grabbed at the chance to learn.

"Oh, Dorothy, could you do that?"

"Sure, Barb, I'd be glad to."

Their meeting the following Tuesday evening was very helpful to Barb. They came up with another item for prayer, and decided to meet the following week to discuss it further. After a few weeks of pursuing this informal proce- dure, Dorothy suggested that they plan to do this on a regular basis.

By now Barb saw the value of their meetings, so she gladly agreed to have someone help her grow in Christ.

In a few weeks, the relationship was blossoming because God was working in it. Dorothy looked for other ways to serve Barb, such as meeting her parents who were both unbelievers. Then one day Barb offered to do some- thing for Dorothy. She found a way to serve the one who had served her. This development was significant, because being needed is an integral part of any friendship. This turnabout led to Barb's assuming a giving role, and that was very healthy. She was receiving from her shepherd-mentor, but she was also giving.

SHEPHERDING

In the literal sense, a shepherd is a keeper of sheep—one who herds sheep. In the spiritual sense, a shepherd is one who leads, directs, cares for followers. A mentor is a wise and trusted teacher or guide. In a recent study of mentoring relationships, the authors defined mentoring as "a relationship in which a person of greater rank or expertise teaches, guides, and develops a novice in an organization or profession. The experience has an unusually beneficial effect on the protégé's personal and professional development."[2]

Spiritual shepherding, or mentoring, requires people who are available to lead and help others in various biblically defined ways. These tasks are described and illustrated in Scripture.

One task of the shepherd is to model Christlikeness. Jesus served His disciples, and then told them to do the same. He even went so far as to say, "Now that you know these things, you will be blessed if you do them" (John 13:17).

Another task of the shepherd is to serve those who are hungry for God, both believers and nonbelievers, by feeding them truth. When Scripture is shared, the enemy is defeated as the truth of God opens the eyes of understanding and directs the steps of life (Psalm 119:105).

Yet another task of the shepherd is to help people be accountable. People are more fruitful in their lives when they know they have to answer for their actions and attitudes.

There are, however, certain limitations that a shepherd is faced with, some of which are very beneficial. Changes of heart, for example, can come only from God, in cooperation with the growing believer. We cannot change each other. The same is true of desire. We can stimulate desire and feed motivation—plant the seeds, so to speak—but only God can cause the seeds to grow. These limitations remove from the laborer the sense of being overburdened. The process of developing laborers is a cooperative venture, not a solo task.

Authority lies ultimately with God, not with people. People may serve as His instruments, but those people have definite limits to observe. We can assist others in the process of decision making, but finalizing decisions should rest with them and God.

The limits of our humanity are both a hindrance and a help. Because we cannot fully understand the past, comprehend the present, or visualize the future, we put ourselves and our ministry to people in the hands of God, who can do all three. Where our wisdom is limited by age, experience, and knowledge, we can call on God for the right kind of help. Our vision for others and for ourselves can be expanded by faith in and obedience to the God of all creation.

NOTES
1. Some good materials on the subject of evangelism:

> *God, Man, and Jesus Christ* (tool for leading evangelistic discussions)
> *Leader's Guide for Evangelistic Bible Studies* (guide for conducting evangelistic study based on Gospel of John)
> *Bridge to Life* (tract with easy-to-understand illustration of the gospel)
> *Confronting Jesus* by John Marsh (book examining who Jesus really is)
> *Evangelism as a Lifestyle* by Jim Petersen (book of thought-provoking insights on evangelism)
> *Evangelism for Our Generation* by Jim Petersen (book of practical ways to make evangelism your lifestyle).

These NavPress materials are available through NavPress, P.O. Box 6000, Colorado Springs, CO 80934 or through your local Christian bookstore. I have also been helped personally by *Out of the Salt Shaker, Into the World* by Rebecca Pippert, published by InterVarsity Press.
2. Elizabeth Alleman, John Cochran, James Doverspike, and Isadore Newman, "Enriching Mentoring Relationships," *The Personnel and Guidance Journal*, February 1984.

FOR PERSONAL DEVELOPMENT

1. Do you have your personal testimony prepared to use in evangelism? If you do, is there someone with whom you can share it this week? If not, why not prepare a three-to-five-minute version that includes before, how, and after you became a Christian?
2. Read 1 Corinthians 13 in three or four translations or paraphrases. What has God done to enable you to love people this way?

CHAPTER FIVE

A Vision and a Plan

The first goal I can remember setting was when I was four years old. "Mother," I said, "I need some new shoes, to get ready for school." The second one that I can recall was during my first year at school. My teacher was trying to help me learn how to spell my name. After the first two days of trying to get nine letters in proper order, I decided to change my name. Elizabeth was simply too hard to write, expecially the z.

For three days I thought and thought about what my name should be. Finally I decided on Joe. Short and to the point. Just right. My goal was met. I carefully deposited the three letters in the upper-right corner of my arithmetic paper, proud of my decision. The unfortunate part of the process was that my goal did not correspond with my teacher's plan. She was not pleased to find my name missing and Joe's appearing. In a few moments my accomplishment had become a source of shame.

As I recall this incident I am reminded of the assertion in Proverbs 16:1 that people have their proposed plans but the Lord has the right answer. Planning is important but the blessing of God is essential. His hands are better able to handle our plans than are anyone else's. He can take our plans and enable us to reach our goals, providing they are within His will.

PLANNING

Jesus charged His disciples to pray for workers and to make disciples.[1] The question that immediately arises is, What is a disciple? Is a disciple the same as a worker, or, as some translations say, a laborer?

The dictionary defines disciple as one who accepts and follows a teacher or a doctrine. One secular example of this would be Plato, a disciple of Socrates. A Christian disciple is a follower of Jesus Christ. The disciples of Jesus were to teach all nations to obey everything He commanded them (Matthew 28:20).

Some Christians accept Christ as the Savior, the bringer of new life, but not as the leader of this new life. In a discipling relationship, the focus should be on helping people to so love and appreciate Jesus Christ that they express their love in obedience—acting in accordance with His teachings.

Before Jesus gave His command to obey, He taught the masses and His men how disciples were to be characterized. These characteristics are foundational in the development of fruitful, functioning disciples.

1. The first characteristic deals with the expenses involved in becoming a disciple. *A disciple places all others, including family and self, second to Christ* (Luke 14:26). This reordering of priorities often takes some time to accomplish because most people don't like to be in second place. In Matthew 19:29 we find the benefits of this sacrifice. We receive much more than we give, for we inherit eternal life.

When I first faced this issue of placing God first, I thought God expected too much. That was because I was facing separation from my dear sister, who was called to be a missionary. Why should I have to live halfway around the world from my sister? We had survived the tumultuous years of growing up together, and now we needed each other—so I thought. Looking back on that time of separation, my sister and I agree that her leaving was not easy. But had she chosen not to leave, the consequences of her disobedience would have far outweighed the benefits of our trying to stay together no matter what.

2. This story leads into a second characteristic of a disciple: *A disciple carries a cross.* A cross in this context is a trial or affliction that helps us die to ourselves. There will always be trials. However, those borne for Jesus' sake are trials of choice. We are engaged in the discipling process when we help people achieve self-denial through their trials.

3. Undoubtedly neither of the first two discipleship characteristics could be developed apart from the one Jesus expressed to certain Jews in John 8:31-32: *"If you*

*hold to my teaching, you are really my disciples. Then
you will know the truth, and the truth will set you free."*
The truth Jesus is referring to here has been preserved for
us in Scripture. It is a truth that we should pass on as we
help others study and apply the Bible.

4. The true mark of a disciple is found in a com-
mandment Jesus gave His disciples: "As I have loved you,
so you must *love one another"* (John 13:34). The standard
by which they were to love each other was His love for them.
In explaining the great value of this love, He said, "All men
will know that you are my disciples if you love one another"
(John 13:35). How could people identify disciples by their
love? Because no other god can produce love.

5. Shortly after exhorting the disciples to love one
another, Jesus gave them another task that would identify
them as His disciples: "This is to my Father's glory, that you
bear much fruit, showing yourselves to be my disciples"
(John 15:8). As the Holy Spirit brings the fruit of love, joy,
and other such positive qualities into our lives, so He brings
the fruit of people into the Kingdom *through* our lives. This
fruit grows as the seed of God's Word is planted, as the
water of our efforts is supplied, and as God causes the
growth: fruit for the Father's glory.

A major part of the goal-setting process is the ability to
anticipate and make provision for future events. We can
better develop our own personal vision for people by discerning the vision Jesus had for His followers.

PERSONAL VISION

A careful look at what Jesus taught His first disciples yields a
list of excellent topics for new believers. (Several Bible-

study series have been developed with these very topics in mind.)² Another source of similar topics can be found in Paul's two letters to the young church at Thessalonica. The combined topics from the Gospels and 1 and 2 Thessalonians fall into two basic categories: attitudes and skills. You may want to insert these topics in your maturation chart (see Chapter 3) in order to help you determine what topics to cover first, second, and so forth. It is important, when teaching spiritual children, to impart foundational truths on which other truths can be built.

One important fact to remember is that different people require different approaches to learning. For instance, one young believer might need more help with the skill of prayer than with the attitude of greed. When a personal prayer life is developed, a foundation has been laid and a resource located for making progress in other skills and attitudes. Our vision for each individual disciple must truly reflect that person's needs.

TRANSLATING SCRIPTURAL TRUTH INTO PERSONAL REALITY

Sandy was a go-getter. By the time she was twenty-four she had climbed high on the corporate ladder of housing development management. Her salary and power far exceeded her initial expectations.

The spiritual side of her life was another story. She was poverty-stricken and powerless when she met Barb. After a few conversations and a time lapse during which God's Spirit worked on Sandy's heart and mind, Barb was able to lead Sandy into God's family.

Shortly after Sandy's new birth, Barb left the city where they both lived, and Shelly became the shepherd through whom Sandy was guided in her growth.

In the establishing process Shelly used several means for getting scriptural truths into Sandy's life. She created an environment for growth by helping Sandy find a church where she received Bible-centered teaching. This gave a sense of authority to God's Word, a new concept to Sandy. To help Sandy appropriate God's Word, Shelly helped her get into a Bible study group where each person came with a prepared lesson to discuss. The participants shared concerns for prayer, verses they had memorized, and lessons recently learned. This group became a significant source of biblical truth and accountability for Sandy.

Shelly also used a one-to-one, personal shepherding approach. She had studied passages like John 15 to discern what basic, foundational truths Sandy needed. She used these essentials (including John 15:7, a verse teaching believers to pray) in a one-to-one planned approach that supplemented the group Bible study. Her lesson plan could have looked like this:

Date:　January 1

Topic:　Prayer

Purpose:　To show Sandy why and how she should ask God for what she needs.

Plan:　1. Briefly explain the purpose of this meeting time.

2. Ask her to read John 15:7 aloud, and then ask her, "As you read this verse, what would you say it means?" Discuss this passage with her.

3. Share the story about needing a different car, and how talking with God about it relieved anxieties and how a good used Datsun was purchased from a friend.

4. Pray briefly together, mostly thanking God but also asking for something that she really needs.

Follow-through: Try to find something daily to talk to God about; include some thanksgiving.

Shelly used this format, adjusting it as needed to fit various topics. Sandy responded positively, learning much. Before long she saw some friends respond to the love of God as she had. Sandy now had living truth in her life.

Jenny was another woman who needed to learn how to make the Bible living and active in her life. She was growing as an adolescent Christian, confronting obstacles to godliness and trying to be obedient. One day she talked to her shepherd about her need for knowing God better.

But how does one know God better? There were a lot of questions in the minds of both of them about what to do. After prayerful consideration, Jenny's mentor, Beth, came up with this plan for her:

Date: March 15

Topic: God's love

Purpose: To study specific aspects of God's love for appreciation and trust.

Plan: 1. Explain the purpose of this time together.
2. Pray for hearts to grasp and apply truth.
3. Go through 1 John, noting all references to God's love.
4. Discuss the evidences and uses of God's love.
5. Pick one verse to memorize this week.

Follow-through: 1. Record some evidence of God's love daily for

one week. Share some notations at the end of
the week.
2. Continue for three more weeks.

Jenny and Beth covered several specific characteristics of God, following this format. Each of them also read
material about God's attributes written by contemporary
authors. The results of these efforts were far more positive
than either person anticipated. Jenny and Beth became
more secure as they comprehended God's love for them.
They became more faithful as they saw God's faithfulness
to them. Jenny moved toward Christian adulthood, and
Beth became a more godly laborer.

COMBINED APPROACHES: UNSTRUCTURED AND RECREATIONAL

I always appreciated the informal times Dottie and I had
together. Cleaning the house, helping her do laundry, setting the table for dinner, or going grocery shopping with
her were special times of learning for me. Even in casual
conversation, I learned many truths through careful
observation.

One incident was particularly interesting. Setting the
table seemed like a small task to me. I was in the habit of
putting the necessary items on as quickly as possible. One
evening when I failed to place the silverware neatly beside
the plates, I was reminded that "everything should be done
in a fitting and orderly way" (1 Corinthians 14:40).

My first response was, "What difference does it make?
They'll be picked up in a minute or so anyway."

Dottie fielded my question most graciously, replying,
"It will let our friends know that we care about them if

everything looks nice and if they are able to pick up the silverware easily."

I pondered that for a moment. She was right. It had never occurred to me to think along those lines. I had always just done what needed to be done, without considering the reason for the work. Two important lessons came from that incident: I learned to consider others more often, and I learned to think about the purposes for doing things. Although I was embarrassed at having to be told how to put silverware on the table, I was very grateful to learn such important lessons.

This unstructured approach could also be used by inserting an extra discussion on a topic in a Bible study group. One good question can lead to a very profitable time of interaction.

Look for ways to interact with people on a casual basis. For example, there are numerous opportunities for modeling and sharing lessons both during and after athletic games. One brief comment on how God enabled us to persevere in playing racquetball for two hours could challenge a growing Christian to relate God's power to daily life.

When Brenda went shopping, she took Amy with her. They prayed over their needs, and then looked for the items on their shopping lists. What fun they had—catching sales, refusing impulses, and buying carefully. After two hours they dropped in at the nearest restaurant, and over a cup of coffee they discussed how God's faithfulness was evidenced in their shopping trip.

If Brenda had simply told Amy how faithful God is rather than illustrating it through experience, the results would have been limited. Amy learned through both Scripture and experience that God is faithful.

Discipling is not an abstract theory or a spiritual board game. It is a personal vision for how to help an individual develop her unique spiritual potential. But every personal vision requires a tailor-made practical plan. Only then can the vision become a dynamic reality in the Kingdom of God. Only then can theory become action.

NOTES
1. Matthew 9:37-38, 28:19.
2. Good studies for new believers:

> *Design for Discipleship* (7-book Bible study series with leader's guide)
> *Beginning with Christ* (booklet on five key assurances)
> *Lessons on Assurance* (companion Bible study for *Beginning with Christ*)
> *Think It Through* by George Howard (follow-up Bible study)
> *Growing in Christ* (excellent practical study for new believers)

These NavPress materials are available through NavPress, P.O. Box 6000, Colorado Springs, CO 80934 or through your local Christian bookstore.

FOR PERSONAL DEVELOPMENT

1. Read Proverbs 16 carefully. Make a list of the principles there that relate to making plans. Think of some ways that you can apply your findings to a current relationship you have with a growing Christian.
2. What are the essential teachings of John 15? Write a prayer of thanksgiving to God for what you learned from one of these teachings that will make your life richer.

CHAPTER SIX

Establishing a Foundation

My mother was quite a resourceful person. She had a high capacity for utilizing what was available to her. Her enterprising, practical approach to life ranged all the way from using cereal-box wax paper as lunch box liners to having us help with various homemaking tasks. She instinctively knew how to capitalize on her opportunities.

The dictionary defines resource as that which is resorted to for aid or support. When prayer is used as a means of turning to God for aid or support, it can be an invaluable resource.

When my youngest sister was seven, one evening she

told me that she could hardly wait until she was nine because then she would be old enough to go to church camp. When I asked her why, she answered, "So I can become a Christian."

My heart skipped a beat. "Would you like to become a Christian now, and not have to wait for another two years?"

She looked at me for a minute, and then asked, "You mean I don't have to wait?"

"No," I responded, trying hard to keep my excitement under control. "You can become a Christian now. Tonight."

"Tonight?"

"Yes, now. Would you like me to show you how?"

"Oh, yes!" she responded. And so we were busy for the next half hour discussing the importance of a commitment to Christ. She received Christ as her Savior that evening.

Because I was a college student living away from home at the time, I was not able to be of much personal help to her subsequent growth. Prayer was the first resource I used. I prayed, "Lord, thank You for Mary Ellen. Please help her hunger for Your Word. Please help her be faithful in her morning devotions with You."

Once after praying this request, I received a letter from Mary Ellen asking for ideas on how to learn from God's Word. As I recall, she was then about eleven years old. I sent her several suggestions, and enlisted the prayers of a couple of my friends. The next time I saw her, I could perceive real growth in Mary Ellen's understanding and application of Scripture.

This combination of prayer and God's Word as resources helps a person learn from a wellspring of inspiration. In Chapter 5 we looked at a story about how Brenda took Amy shopping to help her learn through practical experience. Amy was able to grasp God's faithfulness because Brenda gave her personal input from Scripture, along with dedicated prayer.

PRACTICAL RESOURCES

On one occasion, Brenda asked me to speak on the subject of knowing from Scripture what to do with a new believer. Three Christians she was establishing would benefit from my presentation, so I spoke. I was a personal resource.

Guided experiences are both profitable and fun. After giving a cassette explaining a certain principle to a disciple, I often give an assignment for follow-through. On one occasion, I took a friend to the local library where we found a book that would enlarge her understanding of a topic of interest.

As growth is made in the establishing process, it is increasingly important for the disciple to learn to think of others. We can lead Christians in their concern for non-Christians by having them join us when we are with our nonChristian friends. It often works out for them to participate in some way, either by asking a question or by telling how they put their trust in God through Christ.

Dottie used all the circumstances of my life as resources when she was establishing me. Events, relationships, even traumas served as a means of leading me toward obedience, prayer, fellowship with God, and sharing my faith. Instead of telling me she didn't have time to help me with these issues, Dottie met me where I was and helped to take me where I really wanted to be.

One serious problem, among many others, was the area of finances. I responded readily to the challenge of memorizing Scripture, but memorizing Scripture didn't make my car payments or provide me with rent money. My anxiety level dropped considerably after Dottie helped me work out a sound budget. The less I was distracted by anxiety, the more I was able to focus on God instead of myself. Managing my money more properly thus strengthened my obedience. I came to realize that God wants to help me and guide me in *all* areas of life, not just in the strictly spiritual areas.

When I'm alone, I use my spiritual resources by praying for Rita—that she and Jim will love God with all their hearts. I have a list of items for each married woman who was once part of my establishing ministry. My prayer time for each woman serves three people: It honors God, it helps that woman, and it blesses me. I am blessed because prayer enhances my trust in God, a primary factor in being a successful laborer.

When I am with a woman whom I am establishing in the basics of the faith, I pray *with* her. It doesn't matter if it's part of a planned meeting time or an unstructured time. During the planned, structured times, it is generally more feasible to make use of the Bible, thought-stimulating books, and cassettes. The unstructured times usually lend themselves more to conversations, personal examples, and circumstances.

One caution: Guard against becoming too rigid in any form or method. The more I got to know Patty, the better I was at choosing a method that she could both enjoy and follow. Sometimes we sat on the couch and talked, or went out for tea and talked. Sometimes I had a formal lesson plan in front of us, and at other times it was all in my head and my heart. The variety of methods I used helped to keep her interest and serve as a model of a transferable system for her to use with others.

WITH ONE OR MORE

In some situations, we need to consider ministering to the growing Christian in the context of groups. This method can be very beneficial. If she is in a Bible study group that *you* are leading, she may profit more than she would from one where you are both simply participating. In either case, her relationship with and appreciation for you may help her be more vulnerable in the group.

Ruth and Nancy were two women I was earnestly trying to develop as laborers. On one occasion I asked them to be prepared to share some highlights from the books they were then reading. To provide a pleasant atmosphere, we drove out of the city to a very nice historic park. After enjoying our picnic lunch together, we shared our highlights and talked about our books. All three of us learned a great deal and came to new points in our relationships.

Many good discussions can follow a movie, lecture, concert, play, or other social event. A bridal shower or birthday party can be either preceded or followed by an informal talk about God's love, faithfulness, or some other trait. The possibilities are endless, the benefits eternal.

These practical resources need to be encompassed by the leading, enabling Spirit of God. Only He can prevail in the tug of war created by our archenemy of growth. The enemy would say, "No one has time to do these things. Send these women to church so that you can get busy at more important things, like your own Bible studies."

Our studies are necessary, but we also need to *apply* the teachings we encounter. Too much studying without exercising our findings can result in spiritual obesity. Such mental corpulence neither honors God nor serves people.

CONCERNS

I have observed that many people are concerned about not having the skills, resources, or confidence to become effective laborers. My own initial fears were centered in all three of these areas. One issue became clear, however, as I studied the Bible. Skills in discipling are not emphasized in the New Testament, but heart and character are. When Paul was instructing the Colossians about who Christ was and what He had done, he expressed his own approach to discipling: "So, naturally, we proclaim Christ! We warn everyone we meet, and we teach everyone we can, all that we know about him, so that we may bring every man up to his full maturity in Christ. This is what I am working and struggling at, with all the strength that God puts into me" (Colossians 1:28-29, PH).

This passage reveals a few important facts about Paul's purpose and vision:

1. Paul's ministry was not a solo venture, but he was part of a team effort.

2. Paul and his team members taught whomever they could. But there were limits to what was accomplished.

3. He taught what he knew. His own knowledge and awareness had a great bearing on his message.

4. He had a purpose in sight: to bring people up to their full maturity in Christ. His purpose was the foundation for his action.

5. He worked at his task with strength from God. What God asked him to do, God helped him to do.

When I closely examined 1 Corinthians 2:1-5, I found similar concepts. The *Phillips* paraphrase renders 2:5, "Plainly God's purpose was that your faith should rest not upon man's cleverness but upon the power of God."

We can learn skills if we try, if we pray, and if we openly acknowledge to God and other people our own need. We can learn much through experience as we make every effort to observe ourselves in action. Our most important step is the first one: *Try.* Pray, and then try again. And don't wait for perfection.

Some of our meager resources may be due to the time limits of family needs or demanding careers. Perhaps we are fearful of trying to do what no one else around us is doing. Sometimes we face discouragement when we have to look long and hard to find a hungry young believer who will respond to our initiatives of help. Or, what if there is no Christian bookstore nearby? And some people find it very difficult to develop the personal relationship necessary for an establishing ministry.

In order to confront and dispel these shortsighted appraisals of our resources, we need to decide to base our decisions to minister on directives from Scripture, not on exterior circumstances. Neither Naomi nor Priscilla, biblical models of laborers, evaded God's direct call to discipleship. Naomi's investment of life and energies into one woman—God's chosen woman—produced the results that God intended.

The fourth time I enrolled as a university student, I did so in order to lead women to Christ and disciple them. Because I was nearly fifteen years older than most of my classmates, I felt somewhat isolated. In addition to that barrier, my purpose in being there was different from theirs. It seemed that I had no one with whom I could talk, pray, and share my concerns. One Sunday morning I stayed home from church to pray and evaluate my situation. As I sat in the kitchen, head in hands, tears on the table, my heart aching, some words from the Lord returned to my mind: "I will give . . . people in exchange for your life" (Isaiah 43:4). My very next thought was, "Okay, Lord, I'll keep on, as long as You help me."

Within twenty-four hours a young lady walked into the office where I worked part-time and asked me to help her grow. I knew then that God wanted me to persevere in my ministry. Within a few weeks I learned of a returned missionary, who in a few months became my prayer partner. I · saw her as a resource. My prayer friend helped me be more realistic both in what I tried and in what I expected. Her support added to my efforts were far more effective than my efforts alone.

CONFIDENCE

God is not surprised when we lack confidence. Since the days of the Old Testament patriarchs, God has been using His power to help His people. When we focus on His power, we force our fears into oblivion. Reviewing the message of Matthew 28:18-20 will keep our life purpose vitalized. When God's people act on God's message, He instills courage in their hearts, virtually transforming them into instruments for the benefit of others. Trusting God for results enables us to persevere in the present. We are fellow workers with God—by His grace and for His glory.

FOR PERSONAL DEVELOPMENT

1. List some ways that you can make use of prayer as a resource.
2. Pick one of the concerns you have regarding your effec-

tiveness as a laborer. Confront it with Scripture, and come up with a tentative plan for its demise.
3. Express your thanks to God for some of the specific resources you have available for your own growth.

CHAPTER SEVEN

Equipping Women for Service

Patty was responsive throughout the process of becoming *established* as a mature believer (a process that is summarized in Colossians 1:28-29). She had visible evidence in her life of Christlike maturity. She showed love for God and for others (1 Timothy 1:5). She had been trained in distinguishing good from evil, and now she was ready for solid food (Hebrews 5:14).

By the time Patty moved to the city where I lived, she was ready to enter the process of becoming a laborer. She was ready to be *equipped,* or prepared for service (Ephesians 4:12-13). Her spiritual growth was the result of her positive response to certain foundational teachings. Patty's readiness for additional developmental teachings was apparent. Her introductory words to me indicated her open heart and attitude.

She parked her car in front of my house, walked up the steps, and, when I opened the door, said brightly, "I'm here!" Because her arrival was earlier than I had expected, an element of surprise registered in my voice. "So soon?"

But Patty was undaunted, and waited for me to invite her in. Our encounter that day began a process that resulted in Patty's becoming a fruitful laborer.

BECOMING AN EQUIPPER

An equipper is someone who helps a disciple become a laborer—not just growing herself, but helping others grow. Being an equipper takes a certain measure of spiritual gifts and a clear calling, explained in 1 Corinthians 12 and Ephesians 4. In the New Testament there is no passage stating that only certain believers should evangelize, establish, and equip, thus excusing all others. The special calling of *laborer* is given to those people who major on specific training tasks, but is not meant to exclude others from these tasks.

After we have shared our faith with someone, helping her become established in *her* faith, we want to see her do the same with someone else. We want her to have a vision for her own role in multiplying laborers. Paul told Timothy in 2 Timothy 2:2 to entrust what he had learned to those who were "reliable [and] qualified to teach others." Robert Coleman has defined this process as the crucial test of our effectiveness:

Here finally is where we must all evaluate the contribution that our life and witness is making to the supreme purpose of Him who is the Saviour of the world. Are those who have followed us to Christ now leading others to Him and teaching them to make disciples like ourselves? Note, it is not enough to rescue the perishing, though this is imperative; nor is it sufficient to build up new born babes in the faith of Christ, although this too is necessary if the first fruit is to endure; in fact, it is not sufficient just to get them out winning souls, as commendable as this work may be. What really counts in the ultimate perpetuation of our work is the faithfulness with which our converts go out and make leaders out of their converts, not simply more followers. Surely we want to win our generation for Christ, and to do it now, but this is not enough. Our work is never finished until it has assured its continuation in the lives of those redeemed by the Evangel.[1]

This equipping process usually requires more commitment than do the earlier stages of spiritual growth. Certain elements in the process demand more of our time, energy, and resources. Many equippers are greatly affected by the disciple's growth in character, convictions, awareness for ministry, and caring for people. For example, the equipper may have less time than before to spend on her house, to cook, and to do other homemaking tasks. These are sacrifices that affect both people and purse.

Another implication for an equipping ministry is that the specific goals will vary somewhat with each person. The background and depth of the establishing process will affect the defining of goals.

For instance, because Patty had been involved in a thriving outreach ministry before I began equipping her, I didn't have to spend time helping her develop a heart for people. Because I didn't have to teach her the biblical nature of evangelism, I could spend our time in other areas, such as developing relationships, growing in confidence in God, and homemaking.

Many people stop growing before becoming equipped. There are several possible reasons why they stop. First, the relationship between the equipper and the "equippee" must usually deepen, but this can pose a problem. People find these deeper relationships too hard to achieve, and so they give up. For some, the price is too high. On the surface, equipping disciples doesn't seem to be much of a bargain. It is costly to let people know us well enough to learn from our example. Taking time and energy to learn enough to be able to give instruction is expensive. It is costly to bow to Christ as the total Master of our lives.

Along these same lines, availability is another factor in the stunting of spiritual growth. You may want to help someone, but you can't because you have four small children, or an invalid family member, or some pressing obligation. Various personal reasons prevent many equippers from developing disciples into laborers. One that is grievous to me is the lack of vision. Some people do not perceive their potential to equip disciples. It is grievous because it represents two losses: A disciple doesn't become a laborer, and a potential equipper loses the joy of seeing her life enriched through giving to another.

BEGINNING THE PROCESS

The best way to evaluate where to start the equipping process with a disciple is by envisioning that person's growth potential from Scripture. Paul gave us a lengthy example of this in 1 Thessalonians 1:2-10, where he simply reminded the Thessalonian believers of what had changed their lives and what they had accomplished. Those same changes are possible for any growing disciple because they are based on the work of God.

When I first started to help Patty, I envisioned certain areas where she would need to grow. After determining the three most important areas (character, convictions, and confidence in God), I made a list that looked something like this:

Character and convictions	Confidence in God
Ephesians 2:10	Daniel 4:35 (His Sovereignty)
Romans 12:3-21	1 John 3:1 (His Love)
Romans 5:3-5	Isaiah 40 (His Power)
Colossians 1:9-11	1 Thessalonians 5:24 (His Faithfulness)

After preparing this list, I worked at enhancing our relationship. We had fun together. We prayed together. And there were sometimes acts of kindness, such as one morning in early winter. During rush hour traffic, I drove behind her disabled car with my flashers on, moving an incredible five miles per hour. The service manager looked in amazement when she entered the garage off the busy street. "That took courage," he told Patty. We both agreed with him.

Along with such deeds of kindness, I tried to follow the instructions of 1 Thessalonians 2:10-12—to have irreproachable behavior, to encourage, and to admonish. Patty and I had some honest exchanges of ideas, hopes, and dreams. We were not always perfect, but God honored our efforts, both hers and mine.

I thought carefully about possible alternatives to doing this ministry. And I thought seriously about a statement by the nineteenth-century theologian A. B. Bruce:

> The yoke of love which binds us to our fellows is sometimes not easy, and the burden of caring for them not light; but, on the whole, it is better and nobler to be a drudge and a slave at the bidding of love, than to be a free man through the emancipating power of selfishness. . . . A life on the ocean wave, a life in the woods, a life in the mountains or in the clouds, may be fine to dream and sing of; but the only life out of which genuine heroism and poetry comes, is that which is spent on this solid prosaic earth in the lowly work of doing good.[2]

I realized that my life could write that kind of poetry every day, giving myself to doing the good work of helping as many Pattys as possible to become functioning laborers.

ENRICHING THE SUPPLY HOUSE

If we think of our potential laborer as a supply house, then we can concentrate on what we should deliver to her—our *content* for the equipping process. We could use two kinds of baskets to carry our supplies. One is a sewing basket; the other contains first-aid supplies. From the sewing basket we can make pretty items; from the first-aid supplies we can repair aches and pains.

These baskets can illustrate the positive and negative categories of content for equipping. The positives are concepts such as character building and confidence in God. The negatives are problems—poor social relationships, emotional scars, and so forth.

One positive element we can develop is ministry skills. There are several skills that are important for a disciple to learn in order to become a laborer. For instance, teaching others how to share Christ with friends and family is one important skill.

A second skill is how to teach a disciple to establish a new believer. She may be able to use certain abilities and knowledge from her own experience, but there are some areas where she will need to be taught. How to lead a small group Bible discussion or a prayer group is a skill she should definitely learn.

A second arena of positives is the home. If the disciple's home is to be available to others in her ministry, then she will profit from some teachings on relationships, domestic skills such as cooking and decorating, budgeting—anything that will make her home a place where people can see Jesus Christ in real everyday life. As she learns to use her home for outreach ideas, she will greatly increase the possibilities of her witnessing in a natural setting.

AN EXAMPLE

Before Shelly established her own home, she closely observed mine. Since she lived with me for two years, she became well acquainted with how I made my home available. When she and her three housemates began to establish their home, they discussed their purposes and goals, agreeing on some common ones.

One of their goals was to make friends with as many

people as possible in their apartment complex. With this built-in access to nonbelievers, they hoped to witness to and serve many people. They did several creative things to make friends: a garage sale in the basement of their townhouse; a kitchenware party; a cookie exchange Christmas party. They also tried to be friendly whenever the opportunities arose.

Having learned from these experiences, all four women are now using their respective homes to serve God. Their time of being equipped was fruitful.

The context of home is also useful for teaching the character of God, a vital aspect of equipping content. When someone breaks a special possession, we can demonstrate mercy or justice, whichever is appropriate.

DEALING WITH PROBLEMS

Not all of us are trained counselors. But when we become closely involved in helping people, we may uncover special needs or problems. In our modern secularized world, there is an increasing breakdown of moral standards. This places a heavy burden on a laborer, because even when people are forgiven, they still bear deep scars. Quick answers are rarely appropriate, and very few people feel qualified to give advice. The following suggestions on counseling have proved helpful to me.

1. Deal with problems as they arise, but also keep working on the positives. For example, discussing conflicts at home may be necessary, but use the discussion to understand more of God's sovereignty, mercy, faithfulness, or power. Avoid majoring on problems.

2. Deal with past history in view of God's power,

requirements, and desires. For example, God can help us forget that we stole some money because He wants us to cast all our anxiety on Him, because He cares for us (1 Peter 5:7).

3. Confront blatant sin, but do so in the framework of love. Insist on actions to correct the situation, but remain helpful and supportive.

4. Don't forget that you are not totally responsible. Let God take care of people. Leave their emotional and social needs with Him through your prayers. Memorizing Philippians 4:6-7 is a special help in this area. Do what you can, and then leave the results with God, and with the individual you are helping.

NOTES
1. Robert E. Coleman, *The Master Plan of Evangelism*, pages 109-110. This short book is a very good presentation on the subject of reaching the world for Christ through spiritual multiplication.
2. A. B. Bruce, *The Training of the Twelve* (Grand Rapids: Kregel, 1971), pages 522-523.

FOR PERSONAL DEVELOPMENT

1. Is there a skill referred to in this chapter that you would like to be better equipped to do? If so, what can you do and to whom can you go for assistance?
2. Think of some additional references to use in the categories of character, convictions, and confidence in God.
3. List the most important domestic skills for laborers. How would you teach them?

CHAPTER EIGHT

The Materials and the Means

As I was studying American history one day, I came to the account of the 1849 Gold Rush in California. I stopped reading at one point to reflect on what the West would have been like without the unearthing of all that gold. It was a magnificent treasure that went untapped for such a long period of time. Some disciples are like pre-1849 California: rich, but unknown. Their wealth of potential lies buried, latent, undiscovered. This great personal wealth can be uncovered as we work with spiritually hibernating disciples—and God—to develop ministry skills.

CONTENT AND PROCEDURES

If you're helping someone learn to teach the skill of evangelism, find an easy-to-understand book on the subject, and go through it together. (Paul Little's book *How to Give Away Your Faith*, published by InterVarsity Press, is very useful.) It is also vitally important to learn how to study scriptural examples. The following questions are samples of how to probe more deeply into the biblical—and therefore natural—way to evangelize: What exactly did Jesus tell the man in John 3 and the woman in John 4? What did Paul tell the Romans? What basic points did Paul make in Acts 22 as he gave his conversion testimony to the crowd? What was the substance of his conversion in Acts 9?

I ask myself the question, "What do people need to *know*, and what do they need to *do*?" As we read the accounts of Jesus calling people to Himself, we find that He kept it very simple and very direct. Jesus did two basic things when He began His ministry and proclaimed, "Repent, for the kingdom of heaven is near" (Matthew 4:12-17): He showed that He cared, and He asked for a change. Repeatedly this approach is used: caring and communicating.

There are other good approaches for helping a disciple learn to teach another disciple how to share her faith in a way that is natural for her. You could go to some church's evangelistic training session with her (after assuring yourself first that the training is biblical and helpful). After the training session, you could have a discussion on how to use certain materials and ideas to teach someone else. Or you could help to organize a special evangelism training time for women in your church, making sure that your disciple attends.

A POSSIBLE SITUATION

Assume that your efforts to develop your disciple's ability to teach evangelism skills have been helpful. A phone call reveals that the woman she is discipling just helped her neighbor become a Christian. "What do I do next?" she asks. We are now at the second item in the sewing basket: equipping. Doing the work of establishing is one thing; teaching someone else to establish is quite another. Now we need to help one person help another.

Going on the valid assumption that people keep more of what they discover than of what they are told, ask yourself, "What does she know already that she hasn't discovered she knows?" When Dottie first helped me help Janet, she posed this question: "What are the most important things Janet needs to know?"

"Well," I replied, "she needs to know for certain that she is truly a Christian. Unless she knows that, she will always be questioning her relationship with God."

"That's a good start. What else?"

"She needs to know how to talk to God, and how to listen to God."

"Could you help her do those two things?" she questioned.

"Yes," I answered, "I can teach her how to read, study, and apply God's Word, and how to pray to Him."

With these three clarified topics, I began helping Janet. After I had done this informally with Janet, I used the same ideas with other women. Further into the relationship, I would write out lesson plans to use, modifying them to meet the uniqueness of each situation. Almost any given equipping situation could start with the approach I used with Janet.

The whole purpose of equipping is to assist in the process of developing God's people so that they may do His works of service. These works must enable the Body of Christ to function as a smoothly operating organism, not as a headquarters for individuals who have no relationship with each other. We are members of one another with responsibilities that go with this membership. A review of Ephesians 4 always helps me keep this concept in perspective.

The following chart is a sample plan on how to teach a disciple to establish—not all-inclusive in topic, content, or method, but an introduction to three categories of skills.

Topic	Content	Method
I. Ministry skills		
A. Evangelism	1. The gospel 2. Decision to turn to Christ	1. Study Rosalind Rinker's book *You Can Witness with Confidence*[1] for three months (in a group or individually).
B. Leading evangelistic studies	1. Group dynamics 2. Helping people discover and respond to the gospel	1. Use *How to Lead Small Group Bible Studies*[2] for two months in one-to-one time.
C. Leading Bible studies for growth	1. Group dynamics 2. Asking questions	1. Discuss lessons from study group.

Topic	Content	Method
	3. Summarizing	2. List areas of leading.
		3. Practice on each other.
		4. Read book on leading discussions.
D. Leading prayer groups	1. Group dynamics	1. State purpose.
	2. Organizing a group session	2. Outline plan and time schedule.
	3. Prayer	3. Plan for conclusion.
II. Character		
A. Drawing on God's character	1. God's eternality, sovereignty, omniscience, etc.	1. See suggested plan in Chapter 4.
B. Fruits of the Spirit	1. Galatians 5:22-23	1. Do a short topical study on each quality. Clarify job descriptions for the disciple, God the Father, and the Holy Spirit.
C. Relationships with people	1. 1 Corinthians 13	1. Study in depth; memorize the chapter.

Topic	Content	Method
III. Home management		
A. Relationships	1. Ephesians 4-6	1. Study carefully. 2. Memorize key verses.
B. Budgeting	1. Purposes and resources	1. Clarify purpose of money.
C. Outreach	1. Purpose of home 2. Available material items	1. State purposes. 2. Identify potential people to minister to. 3. Make a long-term and short-term plan.
D. Domestic skills	1. Laundry, cooking, cleaning, etc.	1. Work on one at a time. Get tips from local university extension agents, etc.
E. Decorating	1. Color, efficiency, décor choice 2. Items to pray for 3. Things to give away	1. Discuss purpose. 2. Evaluate the items in Content section.

One important concept to remember is that we are not totally responsible for equipping anyone. A disciple grows when the efforts of God, the equipper, and the receiver are combined. These plans for equipping women will take some time to implement. I have realized that not all of the topics need to be covered by me. Others have finished what I began with some of the women I've helped. And some women have the deep heart commitment and essential learning abilities to learn a lot on their own. But an organized plan that includes topic, content, and method (as in the chart above) is an indispensable guideline throughout the whole equipping process.

SUGGESTIONS

The following general ideas have helped me as I have developed disciples. There is no particular order in this list.

1. Take advantage of events in the community, thus saving time and providing variety and balance. For example: (a) counselor training and participation in area-wide evangelistic campaigns; (b) going with the disciple and a friend to a movie that depicts a theme worth discussing.

2. Sponsor a small prayer breakfast that will emphasize the ACTS of prayer: Adoration, Confession, Thanksgiving, and Supplication.

3. Ask a local businesswoman to present her product or skill. This can be useful for building relationships for evangelism.

4. Meet every two weeks to spend an hour reading and discussing select chapters from a book or from magazine articles in order to learn a skill for homemaking.

5. Get a map of your city, county, state, etc., and pray together for unsaved people, pastors, families, schoolteachers, teenagers, college students, and government authorities. This kind of approach to prayer develops heart and vision.

6. Use informal situations to recount how you learned to grow in the areas of personal character addressed in Galatians 5:22-23 and Matthew 5:1-12.

7. Help a disciple have an evangelistic outreach party in her neighborhood: block party, cookie exchange, Valentine's Day party, etc.

8. Meet a disciple for lunch with one of her fellow employees with whom you can share your testimony, complementing her witness. Evaluate this encounter later.

In the field of counseling, the phrase "termination of counseling" is used to describe the point at which the counselor stops meeting regularly with the counselee. The process of equipping also comes to an end, although from observing the Scripture and my own experience, I've noticed that the relationships and contributions may continue long after the planned portion is concluded.

The factors will vary with each equipper and laborer, but several evidences that the disciple has become a laborer should be observable. If she is involved in the process of evangelizing the unsaved and establishing converts, she has been equipped. On the other hand, if she has failed to respond to growth in personal character, she will probably not want to share her faith. Or, if her affairs at home are chaotic or unChristlike, she will probably be too preoccupied to give herself to others. A clearcut evidence that a person is a laborer is that she labors.

Second, when a laborer is ready to venture out on her own, she will usually communicate her readiness. I've observed that at that point there are usually fewer questions, probably because she has so many ideas of her own that she would like to try out. This is a positive, observable step in the process of equipping.

The harvest is plentiful but the workers few. Jesus told

us in Matthew 9:38 to "ask the Lord of the harvest, therefore, to send out workers into his harvest field." When people are ready to go, we need to pray them out.

NOTES
1. Rosalind Rinker, *You Can Witness with Confidence* (Grand Rapids: Zondervan, 1962).
2. *How to Lead Small Group Bible Studies* (Colorado Springs: NavPress, 1974).

FOR PERSONAL DEVELOPMENT

1. As you read this chapter, what was the most encouraging thought that you read? The least encouraging? How can you profit from both?
2. Replace or supplement any references or book suggestions in this chapter with ones you have found helpful and would prefer using.

CHAPTER NINE

The Cost of Your Commitment

She probably had some idea of the chances she was taking. She knew there would be dangers to face, risks to withstand, and obstacles to overcome. She was not particularly adventuresome, but the hazards of discipling women never stopped her. She faced them just as a golf pro faces a tournament—with courage, and as a challenge.

Dottie prayed over those hazards that stood in the way as she labored to bring me along the path of growth. She confronted all obstacles. Her heart overruled her fears in her ministry to my life.

A hazard is defined as a chance, danger, or risk. On a

golf course it is an obstacle, and obstacles are the same as impediments. After pondering these meanings, I drew the following conclusions:

1. Many hazards or obstacles are beyond my control. I've tried to pretend that a certain water hole on a golf course doesn't exist, but it always does. I cannot control the design of the course; I can only adjust to it.

2. Each hazard can stimulate my thinking to some creative, decisive action. Confrontations or conflicts often produce great insights and growth.

3. Some obstacles may be of my own making. Perfectionism—a self-imposed standard of excellence that is set up at the expense of something highly valued—is a definite impediment.

4. My attitude may determine whether the obstacle will be a benefit or distraction. A positive attitude usually generates better responses.

5. God allows obstacles. I found in Proverbs 20:24 that since He directs my steps, I can trust Him to help me meet the challenges that obstacles bring.

OBSTACLES IN THE WAY

The biggest obstacle I usually have to face is myself. Others have told me that they have made the same observation about themselves. There are several things about us that can impede progress. Our feelings, past experiences, and biases prevent our acceptance of certain people for who they are. In some cases, our narrow perspective on life leads us to become impatient with people who are different. Sometimes the fact that we have been undisciplined or neglected may lead to our being weak in relationships.

Often our own insecurities create in us a fear of letting people fail as we are discipling them. Sometimes we tell too much, instead of letting discovery be our method. And we may sometimes lose the impact of a positive issue by over-emphasizing a negative issue.

The potential for good in the obstacles relating to ourselves is great. Our growth can demonstrate the sovereignty of God, showing the potential worth and uniqueness of every individual as we become trophies of God's grace. In 2 Corinthians 1:4 we learn that we are comforted in order to be comforters. As we face difficult issues in our own lives, we more readily understand others who experience these same obstacles.

The second major hazard I've discovered is contained in the words and actions of people not involved in the ministry, such as family members, friends, or teachers. They can hurt our feelings, denounce God, and cloud our objectives. Consider, for example, a nonbelieving father who criticizes his daughter about how she uses her time and money. The following is a true story.

I knew a university student who was excelling at a certain sport. She was chosen to represent her school in an approaching meet. Before the weekend came, she decided to withdraw from the team in order to be more available for personal instruction and group activities that would develop her relationship with the Lord.

When her parents learned of her decision, they told her not to come home any more, even though she was financially responsible for her own education and had been allowed to make other major decisions. They were ashamed of her choice.

This student experienced an important test in this values conflict with her parents, and through this test she saw her faith richly developed. The risk she took that led to her difficulty was well worth the cost. She saw her convictions established, and she became more motivated than ever before to study and memorize God's Word. Without the Word of God to guide her, she would have stumbled.

This victory also gave her a big deposit for her memory bank. As she learned to know God—and see Him answer prayer—she had a strong reserve to draw on during the hard months that followed.

A third hazard in the course of laboring is the area of uncertainty in the woman who is being discipled. Some of her past experiences are unknown to us. When she responds to Scripture or suggestions in certain ways, we are surprised, and understandably so. Significant people in her life may have had strong influences on her. For instance, her unfulfilled mother may have been domineering, or a tactless teacher may have humiliated her. It takes time to learn the reasons behind certain actions, and in some cases we may never learn the reasons.

One area of uncertainty that is evident as we help people is their potential. We don't know immediately God's plan for their lives, nor do we know their hidden needs.

The honesty factor is another risk to be taken in discipling women. You may not know for a long time if the woman you are discipling is really applying the truth that is being taught. Judas wasn't entirely honest with Jesus, nor are many of the people who enter the arena of discipleship.

Difficult as these uncertainties can be, they do hold potential for good. As we assist in the discipling process, we invariably see women's lives become examples of how God overcomes the power of the enemy.

OVERCOMING THE HAZARDS

When Dottie embarked on the role of being my mentor, she faced a person with many difficulties. My despair over life in general had at its core a bitterness at God for having allowed me to suffer—most unjustly, I was convinced. My feelings had been hurt deeply in two job failures. God's love for me was obstructed by my responses to the words and actions of others.

The steps Dottie took me through look so simple on paper, but they were profound in my life. Step one was for me to face reality—to acknowledge what I thought and felt. Step two was to forgive my offenders, and to begin majoring on God for what I had and was, instead of dwelling on the past. Step three was to set some objectives, and to review the ones I already had, including promises to pray about. The purpose of these steps was to help me cooperate with God and to set my sights forward, not backward.

It was almost like a new birth to me. Working through my obstacles took a lot of Dottie's energy and time, but it gave me new hope for life.

A workable beginning in overcoming hazards is to recognize that we as disciplers are born, taught, and led by the Spirit of God. We are not only disciplers, but also learners. We need to go beyond giving help. Sometimes we need to ask others for help. And after we receive help from God, we should say thanks for all the experiences that come to us, even the difficult ones.

The third hazard—areas of uncertainties—is difficult, but not beyond the reach of God. If I don't know the woman I'm discipling very well, I try to be a good listener, asking a lot of questions, in order to get to know her. This process takes time, but it is very profitable.

THE COST

The cost of laboring is a hazard that can be viewed from two basic vantage points: Jesus' perspective and the other alternatives. One afternoon I spent several hours studying Luke 14:25-35 to examine Jesus' perspective on the cost of discipleship and laboring. (Matthew 10:34-42, 16:24-27, and 19:23-30 also address these two issues.)

I was stunned to discover that although multitudes followed Jesus, few counted the cost—and undoubtedly fewer paid the cost. This discovery motivated me to pray for the necessary resources to pay any price to serve God. When I studied the same passage in more detail to learn about the cost concept, I found these four costs for the laborer: (1) Love Christ more than anyone else; (2) Carry your cross—an instrument for death of self; (3) Give all your possessions to God; (4) Keep life "salty" (Matthew 5:13).

Then I listed the other basic alternatives: (1) Love family most; (2) Love self most; (3) Hang on to your possessions; (4) Lose the salt of life. I was greatly challenged by this study to resolve with my heart and mind to pay the necessary cost for discipling women. I am convinced from other passages of Scripture that God will *help* me do everything He *asks* me to do.

There have been many struggles, and probably always will be. But whenever I compare the costs with the alternatives, my conclusions remain the same: The potential for good in paying the price far outweighs the results of choosing the alternatives. God is exalted, and my own life becomes more satisfying as people are helped.

The best way to overcome the hazard of the cost of laboring is to pay the price, enabled by God's leading—and power.

One Old Testament verse from the book of Ruth has been a key motivational force for me as I have tried to pay the costs. "May the LORD repay you for what you have done. May you be richly rewarded by the LORD, the God of Israel, under whose wings you have come to take refuge" (Ruth 2:12). I don't pay the cost in order to receive a reward, but I do know that my depleted resources will be graciously restocked by the God of all riches.

FOR PERSONAL DEVELOPMENT

1. In this chapter we discussed hazards to discipling. Make a chart that summarizes the chapter, using these headings:

	Hazards	
What are they?	Potential for good	How to overcome

2. Add your own suggestions to the list of hazards in this chapter.
3. As you look back on the chapter, what lesson or principle are you most grateful for?

CHAPTER TEN

The Rewards

It's not bribery. It's given in return for certain labor done. It's an expected result of living up to an agreement. Sometimes it's an unexpected bonus.

The concept of *reward* came from God. I cherish this concept, because in certain areas a reward motivates me to keep faithful. At other times, it is a pleasant surprise.

When I was teaching school, one of my favorite tasks was to reward someone for something accomplished. One unforgettable reward for a class of sixth graders was given for winning a softball tournament. I had coached the children diligently, inwardly never expecting to win because

107

our opposition was being led by a bona fide coach. When we defeated them, our greatest reward was the sense of accomplishment. This event helped me understand how much joy God experiences when He rewards us.

When Paul was addressing some unhealthy divisions in the Corinthian church, he included some helpful thoughts about the rewards of ministry. He first used an agricultural illustration (1 Corinthians 3:8), stating that the persons who plant and water are both rewarded according to their own labor. Paul was referring here to *spiritual* agriculture.

In the next section, Paul used the illustration of putting together a building. He explained the vital importance of certain aspects of the building. Note 1 Corinthians 3:14: "If what he has built survives, he will receive his reward." The telling contrast is in verse 15: The loser's work is burned up.

God rewards the person who does the building. In 1 Corinthians 4:5 Paul pointed out that at the Lord's return, certain things will take place. "He will bring to light what is hidden in darkness and will expose the motives of men's hearts. At that time each will receive his praise from God." Those who have served God will stand in His presence and receive His praise. Earth offers no reward that in any way compares to God's. His approval surpasses all else. Two references explain why God's rewards are superior: 1 Corinthians 9:25 and 1 Peter 5:4. His rewards are superior because the crown we receive from Him is imperishable—a never-fading crown of glory.

DISCERNIBLE RESULTS

Napoleon sat down and cried when he thought he had no more worlds to conquer. A famous Hollywood actress committed suicide at the age of thirty because all her goals had been reached and she lacked a purpose for living. But in stark contrast stands the one who labors for—and with—Jesus Christ. One of my first joys when I set my heart to fulfill God's purposes and contribute to His pleasure was a personal sense of meaning. True significance is a deep reward for the work of discipling women.

Great armies have been unable to destroy the power of the gospel as it has been persistently carried, down through history, person to person. When I read of Gladys Aylward's persistence, I recognized that the triumph of right over might is a reward of laboring for God. There are several illustrations of this phenomenon in her biography. In Gladys's life, the right of the gospel triumphed over the might of evil.

Obedience to God brings freedom. The defiant enemy propagates the false message that freedom is self-expression. But when we obey God and help fulfill His Great Commission to the world, we have freedom in its truest sense. This freedom disallows the claims of self-centeredness. The self in us will always clamor for respect, attention, and rights. But it is in giving that we receive, when the giving is to Christ. This rewarded freedom to give allows us to die in order to bring forth many new lives.

One reward of great promise is that our righteous works will last (1 Corinthians 3:14). When I was a university student, I met Marcia, who was a freshman and a young believer. I was able to be her shepherd, assisting in her growth to maturity. After she graduated from the university, she led a Bible study with some university students. A somewhat radical Barb was very interested, and eventually became a Christian. She grew, and made herself available for the establishing process. She moved several times in order to receive further help and also to serve. Among her lasting fruit was Jill, a student at another university. Barb later served three years as a missionary to young women in West Germany, and Jill served one year in France as a short-term missionary. Both are currently involved in reaching young people. They are living works that have lasted.

A great reward mentioned in the New Testament by both Paul and John is that *people* can be our glory and joy. One summer I led a special seminar that was designed to help women grow in their abilities to communicate evangelistically and in the area of establishing. Participating in the seminar were several women I had personally helped to develop. As I sat listening to their presentations, I became very sobered to realize that these women had grown so very much. My sober amazement led to great joy as I listened to them express God's Word with intelligence, confidence, and clarity.

When I was eighteen, I memorized Daniel 12:3— "Those who are wise will shine like the brightness of the heavens, and those who lead many to righteousness, like the stars for ever and ever." At that time I prayed that God would make me a wise woman—able to lead many to righteousness. What a great reward for our labor—to shine like the stars for ever and ever. We may not immediately understand what this means. But God knows what the reward is. He gives it only after He has enabled us to do what this verse emphasizes so well—lead many to righteousness.

For Personal Development

1. Which of the rewards listed in this chapter appear to be the most attractive to you at this time?
2. List some additional verses from Scripture that will help you understand God's system of rewards. List your observations on these verses.

CHAPTER ELEVEN

The Balance of Power

People who have power sometimes use it for their own benefit, but often at someone else's expense. This abuse of power is evident when we look at history. Genghis Khan would never have become known as the scourge of Asia if he had used his power to benefit the Asians instead of using it to conquer them. Herod searched for ways to utilize his power in order to destroy Jesus—but God used His power to save Him.

In the area of ministering to women, the balance of power is very important. We need to understand that the wisdom of God assists us in discerning what limits we have to reckon with in the discipling process. Without a recognition of these limits, it would be easy to assume too much responsibility.

We also need to have spelled out for us what specific tasks are up to each person. The following four roles clarify the balance of power.

(1) *The indisputable role of the Holy Spirit*—A careful look at John 16:8-11 shows the Spirit to be the Convictor, or Convincer. Only the Holy Spirit could have convinced Barb that she was guilty of sin, in need of righteousness. The opinions of her friends influenced her to believe that her actions and attitudes were acceptable. The Spirit of God convinced her otherwise.

The Holy Spirit also has the role of Guide, making known to growing believers the truth of Scripture. He is also the Helper, and Counselor.

When Barb began to read the Bible, she found words that seemed to have been written especially for her. This transfer of relevance from printed page to hungry heart was made possible by the Holy Spirit, undeniably the best teacher Barb ever had.

(2) *The instrumental role of the shepherd*—The shepherd is to be the teller of truth—the one who communicates in contemporary language to a contemporary audience. When I went to the university where Marcia and Barb were students, I memorized 1 Corinthians 2:1-5 in the *J.B. Phillips* paraphrase because these verses so clearly expressed what I wanted to do during the time I would be there:

> In the same way, my brothers, when I came to proclaim
> to you God's secret purpose, I did not come equipped
> with any brilliance of speech or intellect. You may as well

know now that it was my secret determination to concentrate entirely on Jesus Christ himself and the fact of his death upon the cross. As a matter of fact, in myself I was feeling far from strong; I was nervous and rather shaky. What I said and preached had none of the attractiveness of the clever mind, but it was a demonstration of the power of the Spirit! Plainly God's purpose was that your faith should rest not upon man's cleverness but upon the power of God.

It was from these verses that I saw more clearly than ever before that I was merely a teller, not the author of truth. If people didn't believe, it was the truth they rejected, not me (as long as I was doing the telling in dependence on the Holy Spirit). This concept helped Marcia to be more persistent in trying to help Barb understand her need to believe in Christ.

In the latter stages of establishing and equipping, there is a special freedom as we assume the role of being instruments, not the ultimate authority. This is true because there are variables that are ultimately beyond our control, and yet as instruments we can have a significant influence on them. Here are a few ways of being instruments, gleaned mostly from 1 Thessalonians:

1. Teller of truth
2. Servant (prayer, hospitality, and practical help)
3. Model of Christlikeness
4. Stimulator (to think, work, and plan)

(3) *The indispensable role of the disciple*—As the disciple assumes the role of the learner, she will apply the truth revealed to her by the Spirit. She will do as Paul instructed Timothy: "Reflect on what I am saying, for the Lord will give you insight into all this" (2 Timothy 2:7). If

she wants to learn, you can hardly do anything wrong. If she doesn't want to learn, you can hardly do anything right.

(4) *The immutable role of the sovereign God*—With His supreme power, God brings into being an amalgam of all the efforts. The building of a precious life is the result.

Where people might cause divisions, God brings unity. When a young believer shows evidences of growth, one person might say, "Hey, look at June. She's in my study group. See what I've done for her." The person she makes this statement to bristles and retorts, "Have you forgotten who led her to Christ in the first place? I did." But God has worked through both persons, molding June into a mature structure of grace and love. His portion of the process is necessary to all concerned and most excellent in its effect.

FOR PERSONAL DEVELOPMENT

1. Read carefully 1 Corinthians 3:6-23 and 15:10. Note your observations about the roles of Paul, Apollos, the Corinthians, and God. How do these observations affect your thinking? Your confidence? Your plans for action?
2. As you reflect on this chapter, what are you most grateful for? How can you best express this gratitude?

CHAPTER TWELVE

A Parting
Note

I am a different person now than I was on the day I decided to drive my blue Ford into a tree. When I ask myself how and why I am different, the first answer that comes to me is *because of the work of God.* When I trusted God, He helped me love Him—and others. When I served God by discipling women, He enriched my life.

My desire in this book is to provide a practical guide for discipling women. I pray that you will be challenged to apply the material you have read. I pray, too, that many women will become laborers as a result of the impact of this book. To help you answer my prayers to use this book profitably in the discipling process, I have compiled the following suggestions and thoughts:

1. Review the personal development section for each chapter. Complete anything you left unfinished.
2. Set priorities for any areas of personal growth that you have perceived as needs in your own life as you read this book. Remember that all growth takes time and effort, but also requires that we take a first step.
3. Identify your umbrella for accountability in evangelism, establishing, and equipping. For what people and in what relationships does God want you to be responsible?

I have omitted certain specifics due to the fact that each person is so unique that the discipling process must be somewhat tailored to the individual. I have presented certain principles of Scripture without including all the applications of these principles, knowing that the applications will vary with each person.

Finally, each woman of God can have a special impact on the lives of many other women. Together as women of God's Kingdom we can, with His help and by His grace, reach the world.